George Livermore

An historical research respecting the opinions of the founders of the

Republic

on Negroes as slaves, as citizens, and as soldiers

George Livermore

An historical research respecting the opinions of the founders of the Republic
on Negroes as slaves, as citizens, and as soldiers

ISBN/EAN: 9783744742009

Printed in Europe, USA, Canada, Australia, Japan

Cover: Foto ©ninafisch / pixelio.de

More available books at **www.hansebooks.com**

AN

HISTORICAL RESEARCH

RESPECTING THE

OPINIONS OF THE FOUNDERS OF THE REPUBLIC ON NEGROES AS SLAVES, AS CITIZENS, AND AS SOLDIERS.

READ BEFORE THE MASSACHUSETTS HISTORICAL SOCIETY,

AUGUST 14, 1862.

By GEORGE LIVERMORE.

FOURTH EDITION.

BOSTON:
A. WILLIAMS AND COMPANY,
100, WASHINGTON STREET.
1863.

EXTRACT FROM THE RECORDS.

A stated monthly meeting was held this day, Thursday, August 14th. In the absence of the President (the Hon. ROBERT C. WINTHROP), Colonel THOMAS ASPINWALL, one of the Vice-Presidents, took the chair.

. . . . .

Mr. LIVERMORE communicated a paper (portions of which he had read at the July meeting) "*On the Opinions of the Founders of the Republic* respecting *Negroes* as *Slaves*, as *Citizens*, and as *Soldiers*."

Mr. NORTON moved, That the thanks of the Society be presented to Mr. Livermore, and that a special Committee be appointed to print the paper at the expense of the Society.

Before this motion was put, Mr. LIVERMORE remarked, that he began his research as an individual effort, intending to print a few copies only, for private distribution. He had brought the subject before the Society at the July meeting, that he might receive aid or suggestions from members who were present. At the request of many members of the Society he had extended his investigations; and, as they desired, had now offered the results of his researches. He hoped he might be permitted to carry out his original purpose of printing the paper, at his own expense, for gratuitous distribution. He should, if such was the pleasure of the meeting, print it as a paper read before the Massachusetts Historical Society.

. . . . .

Mr. EVERETT expressed the gratification with which he had listened to a paper containing so much valuable information, and hoped that it might be printed in the manner most agreeable to Mr. Livermore.

He suggested that the motion of Mr. Norton be so modified as to obviate the objections raised by Mr. Livermore. He hoped, if consistent with his plan, that Mr. Livermore would extend his researches so as to include the services of colored seamen in the American Navy. Mr. Everett related an anecdote of an aged slave, the last of his class, showing the mildness of slavery in Massachusetts before its final extinction.

Mr. WATERSTON, Secretary *pro tempore* of the July meeting, said he had made known the proceedings of that meeting to the venerable senior member of the Society, the Hon. Josiah Quincy, who, though unable at present to attend the meetings, retains a deep interest in all the Society's transactions. He had just received from him a letter, which he begged leave to present to the Society: —

"QUINCY, Aug. 9, 1862.

"Rev. R. C. WATERSTON,

"DEAR SIR, — Your letter of this date communicates to me the purpose of Mr. Livermore to collect and publish documents on the subject of Slavery and Negro Soldiers, originating from the great men who were guides of public affairs at the time of the American Revolution. I should regard such a publication as useful and desirable, and I heartily wish Mr. Livermore success; and I shall be happy, according to my means, in aiding him in his purpose.

"In respect to the general subject of slavery, I apprehend he will find very little favorable to the institution among the relics of the great men of that period.

"Disgust at it was so general, as to be little less than universal. Among slaveholders, the language and hope of putting an end to the evil as soon as possible was on all their tongues; but, alas! it was far from being in all their hearts. Some of the leaders saw the advantages derived from it by the unity and identity of action and motive to which it tended, and its effect in making five States move in phalanx over the Free States. They clung to the institution for the sake of power over the other States of the Union; and, while they were open in decrying it, they were assiduous in promoting its interests and extending its influence.

"By constantly declaring a detestation of slavery, they threw dust into the eyes of the people of the Free States; while they never ceased to seize every opportunity to embarrass the measures which would advance the interests of the Free States, and at the same time to strengthen and extend the interests of the Slave States. We can trace their policy in history. We now realize the result.

"With all their pretensions, the leading slaveholders never lost sight, for one moment, of perpetuating its existence and its power.

"Truly and respectfully yours,

"JOSIAH QUINCY."

Mr. WASHBURN spoke with interest of the letter which had just been read, remarkable as coming from a gentleman of such experience, and at so advanced a period of life. He then gave several historical facts which had come to his knowledge when writing his "History of Leicester," corroborating the statement of Mr. Livermore respecting the common practice of using negroes as soldiers during the war of the American Revolution.

The vote thanking Mr. Livermore for his paper, and committing the manuscript to him, to be printed in the manner most agreeable to him, was unanimously adopted.

RICHARD FROTHINGHAM,

Secretary pro tem.

NOTE TO THE THIRD EDITION.

This historical paper is reprinted from the volume of "Proceedings of the Massachusetts Historical Society" for the year 1862–63. It was there printed, with a few alterations, from the original edition which had been issued for private distribution. These alterations are the following : —

1. The extract from the Message of Jefferson Davis is now printed from the "National Intelligencer" of 7 May, 1861, where it purports to be printed in an authentic form. In the first edition there were some errors and omissions in this document, as taken at second hand from the "New Orleans Picayune" of an earlier date.

2. The first paragraph on Dr. Franklin's opinions has been modified by the omission of a statement found to be not correct. The truth of what remains is independent of it.

3. In speaking of the practice of receiving free negroes as soldiers at the commencement of the Revolution, it was not quite correct to state so broadly that they were "enrolled in the militia." The word "militia" was inadvertently used as synonymous with "army." The language of the paragraph has been so altered as to secure verbal accuracy.

4. A sentence affirming the exemption, in Massachusetts, of "Scotchmen," as well as "negroes," from training in 1656, is omitted ; and two or three specific laws are cited, showing the vacillating policy which was pursued on the subject of employing negroes as soldiers in the early legislation of this Colony.

5. The extract from Mr. Sabine's "American Loyalists" is printed from the author's copy, corrected for a second edition of that work. The only important alteration in this extract is the substitution of "other States" for "New England" in the passage relating to the number of soldiers sent to the aid of South Carolina.

6. Only one important addition has been made. Extracts are given from the writings of John Jay, the first Chief Justice of the United States Supreme Court, showing his opinions, contrasted with those of Chief Justice Taney, his latest successor.

Since the publication of the first edition, my attention has been directed to numerous facts and documents illustrating the subject, which I have not used. Many of these ought to be published. It was at one time my purpose to incorporate them in the second edition of this Research; but I found that by so doing I should swell it considerably beyond the customary limits allotted by the Historical Society to such publications. I therefore reserve them for some possible future use. If the requisite leisure can be gained from pressing duties, perhaps these new materials may hereafter be combined with those here presented in preparing a more elaborate and complete history of the subject.

G. L.

Dana Hill, Cambridge,
   May, 1863.

NOTE TO THE FIRST EDITION.

In the reading of the following paper before the Massachusetts Historical Society, many of the documents now printed were necessarily omitted, or but briefly alluded to. In order to make room for these without unduly increasing the size of this pamphlet, some of the remarks in the original paper have been left out. Though the special object of this research was to ascertain the views of the Founders of our Republic, it has been thought pertinent, in relation to the employment of negroes as soldiers, to present also some evidence of the opinions and practice of contemporary British officers in America. Many appropriate documents, equally illustrative of the whole subject, have been passed by; but it is believed that what are given will suffice to show impartially the general state of public sentiment at the time when our Government was established.

G. L.

Boston, October, 1862.

CONTENTS.

II.

OPINIONS OF THE FOUNDERS OF THE REPUBLIC RESPECTING NEGROES AS SOLDIERS.

APPENDIX.

I.

NEGROES AS SLAVES AND AS CITIZENS.

" We *cannot* put the negro out. This remark serves as a complete stopper to all the crimination and recrimination so freely indulged in between parties on the solemn point, — which of the two first brought the negro in. Let them rest quiet hereafter on this topic. The negro was in before they began to talk about him at all. He will stay in, whether they choose to talk about him or not. He will grow in more and more, even while they are sleeping. To deprecate the misfortune is as idle as to complain of the force of the waters of Niagara. The subject is before us; and it is our duty to face the consideration of its proportions like statesmen, and not to imagine, that, if we will only shut our eyes to it, it is not there; still less to suppose that either lamentation or anger, agitation or silence, will in any respect materially change the nature of the great problem which North America is inevitably doomed to solve. From the decree of Divine Providence there is no appeal." — *Speech of the Hon. Charles Francis Adams*, May 31, 1860, in the U. S. House of Representatives.

HISTORICAL RESEARCH.

I.

NEGROES AS SLAVES AND AS CITIZENS.

In this time of our country's trial, when its Constitution, and
even its continued national existence, is in peril, and the people are beginning to be aroused to the magnitude of the work
to be done, all other subjects dwindle into comparative insig-
nificance. Loyal men, of every calling in life, are laying
aside their chosen and accustomed private pursuits, and de-
voting themselves, heart and hand, to the common cause.
As true patriots, then, we, members of the MASSACHUSETTS
HISTORICAL SOCIETY, should do something more than comply,
as good citizens, with all the requirements of the Constitution
and the laws: we must study, in the light of history, and by
the traditions of those who originally founded and at first
administered the Government, the fundamental principles on
which it was based, and the paramount objects for which it
was established. Having done this, it may not be amiss for
us to offer the results of our historical researches to others
not having the leisure or the opportunity to investigate for
themselves. All partisan and personal prejudice should now
be abjured, and all sectional sentiments and views should
yield to the broad and patriotic purpose of ascertaining, as-

serting, and doing our whole duty as citizens of the *United States*, desirous of restoring the Union to its original completeness for its true purpose.

This will not be the first time that our Society has endeavored, from the records of the past, to throw light on the path of the Government in the legislative and military action of the present. We were not long since called together specially to contribute, from an historical point of view, our aid in guiding public opinion; and the publication of the " Report on the Exchange of Prisoners during the American Revolution," read at that meeting, was warmly welcomed, as a timely and serviceable act.

Although there is a wide difference of opinion as to the cause of the rebellion, or rather as to the persons on whom rests the responsibility of having brought on this terrible civil war, yet all are agreed, that, if *negro slavery* had not existed in this country, we should now be in a condition of peace and prosperity.

I have thought that I could not, at this time, perform a more useful duty, as a member of the Society, than by preparing a documentary paper of carefully edited authorities, relating to NEGROES as *slaves*, as *citizens*, and as *soldiers*, — in order to show what were the principles and the practice of the Founders of the Republic, and thus to ascertain who have been unfaithful to the " compromises of the Constitution," and to the principles upon which the Union was based, and for which the Government was established.

In doing this, I shall endeavor to act simply as an historical inquirer, without any attempt to enforce sentiments or theories of my own. It is my purpose to present the simple records of the opinion and action of persons who have acknowledged claims to be considered as authorities.

As an appropriate introduction to the task I have proposed to myself, of producing some of the recorded opinions of those who were eminently the Founders of the Republic, I proceed to set forth, by authentic citations, the modern doctrine which has given occasion for this research, and also some of the most important refutations of that doctrine which have yet appeared.   These, taken together, will exhibit the present state of the great question as to its first two branches; namely, the opinions held in relation to negroes as *slaves* and as *citizens* before, during, and some time after, the formation of the Government of the United States.

It is a noticeable fact, that, while the Southern leaders of the rebellion uniformly denounce the North for having denied to them their guarantied rights under the Constitution, they are widely at variance when they come to specify their grievances.

Mr. Jefferson Davis, on the 29th of April, 1861, in his Message, says : —

" When the several States delegated certain powers to the United-States Congress, a large portion of the laboring population consisted of African slaves, imported into the colonies by the mother-country. In twelve out of the thirteen States, negro slavery existed ; and the right of property in slaves was protected by law.   This property was recognized in the Constitution ; and provision was made against its loss by the escape of the slave.

" The increase in the number of slaves by further importation from Africa was also secured by a clause forbidding Congress to prohibit the slave-trade anterior to a certain date ; and in no clause can there be found any delegation of power to the Congress, authorizing it in any manner to legislate to the prejudice, detriment, or discouragement of the owners of that species of property, or excluding it from the protection of the Government.

" The climate and soil of the Northern States soon proved unpropitious to the continuance of slave-labor ; whilst the converse was the case at the South.   Under the unrestricted free intercourse between the two sections, the Northern States consulted their own interest, by selling their slaves to the South, and prohibiting slavery within their limits.   The South were willing purchasers of a property suitable to their wants, and paid the price of the acquisition without harboring a

(margin note: Jefferson Davis.)

Jefferson Davis.

suspicion that their quiet possession was to be disturbed by those who were inhibited not only by want of constitutional authority, but by good faith as vendors, from disquieting a title emanating from themselves.

"As soon, however, as the Northern States that prohibited African slavery within their limits had reached a number sufficient to give their representation a controlling voice in the Congress, a persistent and organized system of hostile measures against the rights of the owners of slaves in the Southern States was inaugurated, and gradually extended. A continuous series of measures was devised and prosecuted for the purpose of rendering insecure the tenure of property in slaves.

.   .   .   .   .

"With interests of such overwhelming magnitude imperilled, the people of the Southern States were driven by the conduct of the North to the adoption of some course of action to avoid the danger with which they were openly menaced. With this view, the Legislatures of the several States invited the people to select delegates to Conventions to be held for the purpose of determining for themselves what measures were best adapted to meet so alarming a crisis in their history."—*National Intelligencer, Tuesday, 7 May, 1861.*

It is not necessary for us to go out of the so-called Southern Confederacy, nor far from the presence of its pretended President, to refute this accusation of change in principle or in policy on the part of the North.

The associate of Mr. Davis, Mr. Alexander H. Stephens (Vice-President, as he is called,) thus frankly avows his sentiments in a speech, delivered at Savannah on the 21st of March, 1861:—

Alex. H. Stephens.

"The new Constitution has put at rest *for ever* all the agitating questions relating to our peculiar institutions,—African slavery as it exists amongst us, the proper *status* of the negro in our form of civilization. *This was the immediate cause of the late rupture and present revolution.* JEFFERSON, in his forecast, had anticipated this, as the 'rock upon which the old Union would split.' He was right. What was conjecture with him is now a realized fact. But whether he fully comprehended the great truth upon which that great rock *stood and stands*, may be doubted. *The prevailing ideas entertained by him and most of the leading statesmen at the time of the formation of the old Constitu-*

tion, were, that the enslavement of the African was in violation of the Alex. H.
laws of nature; that it was wrong in principle, socially, morally, and Stephens.
politically. It was an evil they knew not well how to deal with; but
the general opinion of the men of that day was, that, somehow or
other in the order of Providence, the institution would be evanescent,
and pass away. This idea, though not incorporated in the Constitution, was the prevailing idea at the time. The Constitution, it is true,
secured every essential guarantee to the institution while it should
last; and hence no argument can be justly used against the constitutional guarantees thus secured, because of the common sentiment of
the day. *Those ideas, however, were fundamentally wrong. They
rested upon the assumption of the equality of races. This was an error.*
It was a sandy foundation; and the idea of a government built upon
it, —when the ' storm came and the wind blew, it *fell.'*

" *Our new government is founded upon exactly the opposite ideas.
Its foundations are laid, its corner-stone rests, upon the great truth, that
the negro is not equal to the white man; that slavery, subordination
to the superior race, is his natural and normal condition. This, our
new government, is the first, in the history of the world, based upon
this great physical, philosophical, and moral truth.* This truth has
been slow in the process of its development, like all other truths
in the various departments of science. It has been so even amongst
us. Many who hear me, perhaps, can recollect well that this truth
was not generally admitted, even within their day." — *National Intelligencer, Tuesday, 2 April,* 1861.

This ought to be sufficient to put at rest for ever the accusation of change of opinion, and of unfaithfulness to the
original compromises of the Constitution and to the spirit of
the founders of our Government. But it is a lamentable fact,
that there are not wanting amongst us men, claiming to be
friends of the Union and the Constitution, who yet, through
ignorance or recklessness, continue to violate the truth of
history on this subject.

Without referring more particularly to political writers
and speakers of this class, I would call attention to the
well-known words of the Chief-Justice of the United-States
Supreme Court, in the celebrated case of Dred Scott, at the
December Term, 1856.

Judge Taney's language is as follows : —

Chief-Justice Taney.

" Can a negro, whose ancestors were imported into this country and sold as slaves, become a member of the political community formed and brought into existence by the Constitution of the United States, and as such become entitled to all the rights, and privileges, and immunities guarantied by that instrument to the citizen? One of which rights is the privilege of suing in a court of the United States in the cases specified in the Constitution.

     .   .   .   .   .

" The question before us is, whether the class of persons described in the plea in abatement compose a portion of this people, and are constituent members of this sovereignty? We think they are not, and that they are not included, and were not intended to be included, under the word ' citizen ' in the Constitution, and can therefore claim none of the rights and privileges which that instrument provides for and secures to citizens of the United States. On the contrary, they were at that time considered as a subordinate and inferior class of beings, who had been subjugated by the dominant race, and, whether emancipated or not, yet remained subject to their authority, and had no rights or privileges but such as those who held the power and the Government might choose to grant them.

     .   .   .   .   .

" They had for more than a century before been regarded as beings of an inferior order, and altogether unfit to associate with the white race, either in social or political relations; and so far inferior, that they had no rights which the white man was bound to respect; and that the negro might justly and lawfully be reduced to slavery for his benefit. He was bought and sold, and treated as an ordinary article of merchandise and traffic, whenever a profit could be made by it. This opinion was at that time fixed and universal in the civilized portion of the white race. It was regarded as an axiom in morals as well as in politics, which no one thought of disputing, or supposed to be open to dispute; and men, in every grade and position in society, daily and habitually acted upon it in their private pursuits, as well as in matters of public concern, without doubting for a moment the correctness of this opinion." — *Howard's Reports*, vol. xix. pp. 403–405, 407.

This remarkable assertion is in direct violation of historic truth. It shocked the moral sentiment of our own community, and excited the indignant rebuke of some of the most eminent Jurists and Statesmen of Europe, who declared the sentiments to be "*so execrable as to be almost incredible.*" It was promptly met and answered by Judge McLean of Ohio, and Judge Curtis of Massachusetts, Associate Justices of the United-States Supreme Court.

Mr. Justice McLean, in his elaborate opinion, says:—

"Slavery is emphatically a State institution. In the ninth section of the first article of the Constitution, it is provided 'that the migration or importation of such persons as any of the States now existing shall think proper to admit, shall not be prohibited by the Congress prior to the year 1808; but a tax, or duty, may be imposed on such importation, not exceeding ten dollars for each person.' *Judge McLean.*

"In the Convention, it was proposed by a committee of eleven to limit the importation of slaves to the year 1800, when Mr. Pinckney moved to extend the time to the year 1808. This motion was carried, — New Hampshire, Massachusetts, Connecticut, Maryland, North Carolina, South Carolina, and Georgia voting in the affirmative; and New Jersey, Pennsylvania, and Virginia, in the negative. In opposition to the motion, Mr. Madison said : 'Twenty years will produce all the mischief that can be apprehended from the liberty to import slaves. So long a term will be more dishonorable to the American character than to say nothing about it in the Constitution.' (Madison Papers.)

.   .   .   .   .

"We need not refer to the mercenary spirit which introduced the infamous traffic in slaves, to show the degradation of negro slavery in our country. This system was imposed upon our colonial settlements by the mother country; and it is due to truth to say, that the commercial colonies and States were chiefly engaged in the traffic. But we know as a historical fact, that James Madison, that great and good man, a leading member in the Federal Convention, was solicitous to guard the language of that instrument so as not to convey the idea that there could be property in man.

"I prefer the lights of Madison, Hamilton, and Jay, as a means of construing the Constitution in all its bearings, rather than to look behind that period into a traffic which is now declared to be piracy, and punished with death by Christian nations. I do not like to draw the sources of our domestic relations from so dark a ground. Our

Judge
McLean.

independence was a great epoch in the history of freedom; and while
I admit the Government was not made especially for the colored race,
yet many of them were citizens of the New-England States, and
exercised the rights of suffrage, when the Constitution was adopted;
and it was not doubted by any intelligent person, that its tendencies
would greatly ameliorate their condition.

"Many of the States, on the adoption of the Constitution, or shortly
afterward, took measures to abolish slavery within their respective
jurisdictions; and it is a well-known fact, that a belief was cherished
by the leading men, South as well as North, that the institution of
slavery would gradually decline, until it would become extinct. The
increased value of slave labor, in the culture of cotton and sugar, prevented the realization of this expectation. Like all other communities
and States, the South were influenced by what they considered to be
their own interests.

"But, if we are to turn our attention to the dark ages of the world,
why confine our view to colored slavery? On the same principles,
white men were made slaves. All slavery has its origin in power,
and is against right." — *Howard's Reports*, vol. xix. pp. 536–538.

The following is a part of the conclusive dissenting opinion of Mr. Justice Curtis: —

Judge
Curtis.

"To determine whether any free persons, descended from Africans
held in slavery, were citizens of the United States under the Confederation, and consequently at the time of the adoption of the Constitution of the United States, it is only necessary to know whether any
such persons were citizens of either of the States under the Confederation, at the time of the adoption of the Constitution.

"Of this there can be no doubt. At the time of the ratification of
the Articles of Confederation, all free native-born inhabitants of the
States of New Hampshire, Massachusetts, New York, New Jersey,
and North Carolina, though descended from African slaves, were not
only citizens of those States, but such of them as had the other
necessary qualifications possessed the franchise of electors, on equal
terms with other citizens.

"The Supreme Court of North Carolina, in the case of the State
vs. Manuel (4 Dev. and Bat., 20), has declared the law of that State on
this subject, in terms which I believe to be as sound law in the other
States I have enumerated, as it was in North Carolina.

" ' According to the laws of this State,' says Judge Gaston, in de- **Judge Gaston cited.** livering the opinion of the court, ' all human beings within it, who are not slaves, fall within one of two classes. Whatever distinctions may have existed in the Roman laws between citizens and free inhabitants, they are unknown to our institutions. Before our Revolution, all free persons born within the dominions of the King of Great Britain, whatever their color or complexion, were native-born British subjects, — those born out of his allegiance were aliens. Slavery did not exist in England, but it did in the British colonies. Slaves were not in legal parlance persons, but property. The moment the incapacity, the disqualification of slavery, was removed, they became persons ; and were then either British subjects, or not British subjects, according as they were or were not born within the allegiance of the British King. Upon the Revolution, no other change took place in the laws of North Carolina than was consequent on the transition from a colony dependent on a European King, to a free and sovereign State. Slaves remained slaves. British subjects in North Carolina became North Carolina freemen. Foreigners, until made members of the State, remained aliens. Slaves, manumitted here, became freemen ; and therefore, if born within North Carolina, are citizens of North Carolina ; and all free persons born within the State are born citizens of the State. The Constitution extended the elective franchise to every freeman who had arrived at the age of twenty-one, and paid a public tax ; and it is a matter of universal notoriety, that, under it, free persons, without regard to color, claimed and exercised the franchise, until it was taken from free men of color a few years since by our amended Constitution.'

. . . . .

" It has been often asserted, that the Constitution was made ex- **Judge Curtis.** clusively by and for the white race. It has already been shown, that, in five of the thirteen original States, colored persons then possessed the elective franchise, and were among those by whom the Constitution was ordained and established. If so, it is not true, in point of fact, that the Constitution was made exclusively by the white race. And that it was made exclusively for the white race is, in my opinion, not only an assumption not warranted by any thing in the Constitution, but contradicted by its opening declaration, that it was ordained and established by the people of the United States, for themselves and their posterity. And, as free colored persons were then citizens of at least five States, and so in every sense part of the people of the United

States, they were among those for whom and whose posterity the Constitution was ordained and established."—*Howard's Reports*, vol. xix. pp. 572, 573, 582.

The Hon. George Bancroft, in his "Oration before the Mayor, Common Council, and Citizens of New York, on the 22d of February, 1862," alluding to the opinion of Judge Taney, notwithstanding his affinities with the political party through which the Chief-Justice was raised to his high station, thus speaks:—

George Bancroft.

"During all these convulsions, the United States stood unchanged, admitting none but the slightest modifications in its charter, and proving itself the most stable government of the civilized world. But at last 'we have fallen on evil days.' 'The propitious smiles of Heaven,' such are the words of Washington, 'can never be expected on a nation that disregards the eternal rules of order and right.' During eleven years of perverse government, those rules were disregarded; and it came to pass that men who should firmly avow the sentiments of Washington, and Jefferson, and Franklin, and Chancellor Livingston, were disfranchised for the public service; that the spotless Chief-Justice whom Washington placed at the head of our Supreme Court could by no possibility have been nominated for that office, or confirmed. Nay, the corrupt influence invaded even the very home of justice. The final decree of the Supreme Court, in its decision on a particular case, must be respected and obeyed: the present Chief-Justice has, on one memorable appeal, accompanied his decision with an impassioned declamation, wherein, with profound immorality, which no one has as yet fully laid bare, treating the people of the United States as a shrew to be tamed by an open scorn of the facts of history, with a dreary industry collecting cases where justice may have slumbered or weakness been oppressed, compensating for want of evidence by confidence of assertion, with a partiality that would have disgraced an advocate neglecting humane decisions of colonial courts and the enduring memorials of colonial statute-books, in his party zeal to prove that the fathers of our country held the negro to have 'no rights which the white man was bound to respect,' he has not only denied the rights of man and the liberties of mankind, but has not left a foothold for the liberty of the white man to rest upon.

"That ill-starred disquisition is the starting-point of this rebellion,

which, for a quarter of a century, had been vainly preparing to raise George
Bancroft.
its head. 'When courts of justice fail, war begins.' The so-called
opinion of Taney, who, I trust, did not intend to hang out the flag of
disunion, that rash offence to the conscious memory of the millions,
upheaved our country with the excitement which swept over those of
us who vainly hoped to preserve a strong and sufficient though narrow
isthmus that might stand between the conflicting floods. No nation
can adopt that judgment as its rule, and live: the judgment has in it
no element of political vitality. I will not say it is an invocation of the
dead past: there never was a past that accepted such opinions. If we
want the opinions received in the days when our Constitution was
framed, we will not take them second-hand from our Chief-Justice:
we will let the men of that day speak for themselves. How will our
American magistrate sink, when arraigned, as he will be, before the
tribunal of humanity! How terrible will be the verdict against him,
when he is put in comparison with Washington's political teacher, the
great Montesquieu, the enlightened magistrate of France, in what are
esteemed the worst days of her monarchy! The argument from the
difference of race which Taney thrusts forward with passionate confidence, as a proof of complete disqualification, is brought forward by
Montesquieu as a scathing satire on all the brood of despots who were
supposed to uphold slavery as tolerable in itself. The rights of MAN-
KIND — that precious word which had no equivalent in the language
of Hindostan, or Judæa, or Greece, or Rome, or any ante-Christian
tongue — found their supporter in Washington and Hamilton, in
Franklin and Livingston, in Otis, George Mason, and Gadsden; in all
the greatest men of our early history. The one rule from which the
makers of our first Confederacy, and then of our national Constitution,
never swerved, is this: to fix no constitutional disability on any one.
Whatever might stand in the way of any man, from opinion, ancestry,
weakness of mind, inferiority or inconvenience of any kind, was itself
not formed into a permanent disfranchisement. The Constitution of
the United States was made under the recognized influence of 'the
eternal rule of order and right'; so that, as far as its jurisdiction extends, it raised at once the numerous class who had been chattels into
the condition of persons: it neither originates nor perpetuates inequality." — *Pulpit and Rostrum*, 1862, pp. 104–107.

In refutation of the common charge, that the North has
changed its position on the subject of slavery, I cannot for-

bear adding an extract from the "Address of the Hon. Edward Everett, delivered in New York, on the 4th of July, 1861." In his own matchless manner, Mr. Everett thus disposes of the whole matter: —

Edward
Everett.

"The Southern theory assumes, that, at the time of the adoption of the Constitution, the same antagonism prevailed as now between the North and South, on the general subject of slavery; that although it existed, to some extent, in all the States but one of the Union, it was a feeble and declining interest at the North, and mainly seated at the South; that the soil and climate of the North were soon found to be unpropitious to slave labor, while the reverse was the case at the South; that the Northern States, in consequence, having from interested motives abolished slavery, sold their slaves to the South; and that then, although the existence of slavery was recognized, and its protection guarantied, by the Constitution, as soon as the Northern States had acquired a controlling voice in Congress, a persistent and organized system of hostile measures against the rights of the owners of slaves in the Southern States was inaugurated, and gradually extended, in violation of the compromises of the Constitution, as well as of the honor and good faith tacitly pledged to the South by the manner in which the North disposed of her slaves.

"Such, in substance, is the statement of Mr. Davis, in his late message; and he then proceeds, seemingly as if rehearsing the acts of this Northern majority in Congress, to refer to the anti-slavery measures of the State Legislatures, to the resolutions of abolition societies, to the passionate appeals of the party press, and to the acts of lawless individuals, during the progress of this unhappy agitation.

"Now, this entire view of the subject, with whatever boldness it is affirmed, and with whatever persistency it is repeated, is destitute of foundation. It is demonstrably at war with the truth of history, and is contradicted by facts known to those now on the stage, or which are matters of recent record. At the time of the adoption of the Constitution, and long afterwards, there was, generally speaking, no sectional difference of opinion between North and South on the subject of slavery. It was in both parts of the country regarded, in the established formula of the day, as 'a social, political, and moral evil.' The general feeling in favor of universal liberty and the rights of man, wrought into fervor in the progress of the Revolution, naturally strengthened the anti-slavery sentiment throughout the Union. It is *the South which has since changed, not the North.* The theory of a change in the Northern mind, growing out of a discovery made soon after 1789, that our soil and climate were unpropitious to slavery (as if the soil and climate then were different from what they had always been), and a consequent sale to the South of the slaves of the North, is purely mythical, — as groundless in fact as it is absurd in statement. I have often asked for the evidence of this last allegation, and I have never found an individual who attempted even to prove it. But however this may be, the South at that time regarded slavery as an evil, though a necessary one, and habitually spoke of it in that light. Its continued existence was supposed to depend on keeping up the African slave-trade ; and South as well as North, Virginia as well as Massachusetts. passed laws to prohibit that traffic: they were, however, before the Revolution, vetoed by the Royal Governors. One of the first acts of the Continental Congress, unanimously subscribed by its members, was an agreement neither to import, nor purchase any slave imported, after the first of December, 1774. In the Declaration of Independence, as originally draughted by Mr. Jefferson, both slavery and the slave-trade were denounced in the most uncompromising language. In 1777, the traffic was forbidden in Virginia, by State law, no longer subject to the veto of Royal Governors. In 1784, an ordinance was reported by Mr. Jefferson to the old Congress, providing that after 1800 there should be no slavery in any Territory ceded or to be ceded to the United States. The ordinance failed at that time to be enacted ; but the same prohibition formed a part, by general consent, of the ordinance of 1787 for the organization of the North-western Territory. In his 'Notes on Virginia,' published in that year, Mr. Jefferson depicted the evils of slavery in terms of fearful import. In the same year, the Constitution was framed. It recognized the existence of slavery ; but the word was carefully excluded from the instrument, and Congress was authorized to abolish the traffic in twenty years. In 1796, Mr. St. George Tucker, law-professor in William and Mary College, in Virginia, published a treatise entitled ' A Dissertation on Slavery, with a Proposal for the Gradual Abolition of it in the State of Virginia.' In the preface to the essay, he speaks of the ' abolition of slavery in this State as an object of the first importance, not only to our moral character and domestic peace, but even to our political salvation.' In 1797, Mr. Pinkney, in the Legislature of Maryland, maintained, that, ' by the eternal principles of justice, no man in the State has a right

Edward Everett.

to hold his slave a single hour.' In 1803, Mr. John Randolph, from a committee on the subject, reported that the prohibition of slavery by the ordinance of 1787 was ' a measure wisely calculated to promote the happiness and prosperity of the North-western States, and to give strength and security to that extensive frontier.' Under Mr. Jefferson, the importation of slaves into the territories of Mississippi and Louisiana was prohibited in advance of the time limited by the Constitution for the interdiction of the slave-trade. When the Missouri restriction was enacted, all the members of Mr. Monroe's Cabinet — Mr. Crawford of Georgia, Mr. Calhoun of South Carolina, and Mr. Wirt of Virginia — concurred with Mr. Monroe in affirming its constitutionality. In 1832, after the Southampton massacre, the evils of slavery were exposed in the Legislature of Virginia, and the expediency of its gradual abolition maintained, in terms as decided as were ever employed by the most uncompromising agitator. A bill for that object was introduced into the Assembly by the grandson of Mr. Jefferson, and warmly supported by distinguished politicians now on the stage. Nay, we have the recent admission of the Vice-President of the seceding Confederacy, that what he calls ' the errors of the past generation,' meaning the anti-slavery sentiments entertained by Southern statesmen, ' still clung to many as late as *twenty years* ago.' " — pp. 31–33.

These extracts from the recorded opinions of the learned associates of the Chief-Justice, the eminent Historian, and the illustrious Statesman and Orator, would seem to furnish a complete refutation of the charges brought against the North of having changed its policy or action, and violated some expressed or implied agreement respecting the supposed sacred and paramount rights of slavery.

But, as historical inquirers, we should not implicitly receive the opinions or assertions of any author, however eminent in position or however impartial in judgment and truthful in statement he may be regarded, without referring to the original records, and comparing the contemporary authorities. It is my purpose to do this, to some extent, at the present time.

The primal American Magna Charta, by which the Founders of the Republic asserted the right of the people to form a constitution and government of their own, was proclaimed on the 4th of July, 1776. Its language is clear and explicit. The authors were men of sense and of learning. They knew the meaning of the words they used. Was it for "glittering generalities" that they pledged their lives, their fortunes, and their sacred honor, or did they regard the sentiments of that immortal document as solemn verities? In those times which tried men's souls, were they guilty of attempting to amuse the fancy by a rhetorical flourish, or, what is worse, to delude their fellow-citizens by the merest cant, or did they intend deliberately and reverently to publish to the world their Political Confession of Faith, and to endeavor to show that faith by their works? *(margin: Declara-. tion of Independence.)*

Happily for us and for the fair fame of those patriots, they have left, in the record of their actions and in their published correspondence, the clearest and most comprehensive commentary on the instrument they signed.

The first article in the National Creed is so broad and universal in its sentiments, that attempts have often been made to narrow its meaning, and limit its application: —

" We hold these truths to be self-evident : that all men are created equal ; that they are endowed by their Creator with certain unalienable Rights; that among these are Life, Liberty, and the pursuit of Happiness ; that, to secure these rights, Governments are instituted among Men, deriving their just powers from the consent of the governed."

It has been truly said by Mr. Bancroft, " The heart of Jefferson in writing the Declaration, and of Congress in adopting it, beat for all humanity : the assertion of right was made for all mankind and all coming generations, without any exception whatever; for the proposition which admits of exceptions can never be self-evident."

The author, it is said, could never have intended to have this language received in its literal significance, for then it

Declara-
tion of
Independ-
ence. would have included in the Declaration persons of African descent; while, at the time of the writing of this document, negro slavery existed in the Colonies, and the author of the paper was himself a slave-holder. Did Mr. Jefferson intend to condemn his own conduct, and that of his associates, by announcing doctrines at variance with their lives?

In Christian morals, the first step towards reformation is a conviction of sin; and the second is confession, and promise of amendment. The patriots and sages who framed our form of government, in declaring their principles as political philosophers, acted in like manner. They did not ignore the fact, that colored men were held in bondage. They did not attempt to conceal, much less to justify, the offence. As, in the popular religious creed of their day, all men, through Adam, had fallen from innocence, and were guilty; so they felt, that, by the act of their ancestors, they were themselves then acting in violation of the natural and immutable laws of political justice.

It should be borne in mind, that the Declaration of Independence is not an ethnological essay, or a disquisition on the physical or intellectual capacity of the various races of men, but a grave announcement of Human Rights.

Mr. Jefferson, in his "Notes on Virginia," has given very fully his views of the physical, moral, and mental capacities of negroes.

Thomas
Jefferson.
"The opinion that they are inferior in the faculties of reason and imagination must be hazarded with great diffidence. To justify a general conclusion, requires many observations, even where the subject may be submitted to the anatomical knife, to optical glasses, to analysis by fire or by solvents. How much more, then, where it is a faculty, not a substance, we are examining; where it eludes the research of all the senses; where the conditions of its existence are various, and variously combined; where the effects of those which are present or absent bid defiance to calculation; let me add, too, as a circumstance of great tenderness, where our conclusion would degrade a whole race of men from the rank in the scale of beings which their Creator

may perhaps have given them! To our reproach it must be said, Thomas Jefferson. that, though for a century and a half we have had under our eyes the races of black and of red men, they have never yet been viewed by us as subjects of natural history. I advance it, therefore, as a suspicion only, that the blacks, whether originally a distinct race, or made distinct by time and circumstances, are inferior to the whites in the endowments both of body and mind." —*Jefferson's Works*, vol. viii. p. 386.

Alluding to these opinions several years afterwards, the author, in a letter addressed to " M. Grégoire, Evêque et Sénateur," says, —

" My doubts were the result of personal observation on the limited sphere of my own State, where the opportunities for the development of their genius were not favorable, and those of exercising it still less so. I expressed them, therefore, with great hesitation ; *but, whatever be their degree of talent, it is no measure of their rights.* Because Sir Isaac Newton was superior to others in understanding, he was not, therefore, lord of the person or property of others. On this subject they are gaining daily in the opinions of nations, and hopeful advances are making towards their re-establishment on an equal footing with the other colors of the human family. I pray you, therefore, to accept my thanks for the many instances you have enabled me to observe of respectable intelligence in that race of men, which cannot fail to have effect in hastening the day of their relief." — *Jefferson's Works*, vol. v. p. 429.

How slavery was regarded at the time is clearly stated in the instructions prepared by Mr. Jefferson for the first delegation of Virginia to Congress, in August, 1774, and printed in a pamphlet form, under the title of "A Summary View of the Rights of British America." I have Italicized a few lines as worthy of particular attention : — ·

" For the most trifling reasons, and sometimes for no conceivable reason at all, his Majesty has rejected laws of the most salutary tendency. *The abolition of domestic slavery is the great object of desire in those Colonies, where it was, unhappily, introduced in their infant state. But, previous to the enfranchisement of the slaves we have, it is*

3

necessary to exclude all further importations from Africa. Yet our repeated attempts to effect this by prohibitions, and by imposing duties which might amount to a prohibition, have been hitherto defeated by his Majesty's negative; thus preferring the immediate advantages of a few British corsairs to the lasting interests of the American States, and to the rights of human nature, deeply wounded by this infamous practice." — *Jefferson's Works*, vol. i. p. 135.

It is well known that some passages in the original draught of the Declaration of Independence were omitted when the paper was finally adopted by Congress. One of these passages shows so strikingly the feelings of the author on this subject, that it may well be cited here: —

" He has waged cruel war against human nature itself, violating its most sacred rights of life and liberty in the persons of a distant people who never offended him; captivating and carrying them into slavery in another hemisphere, or to incur miserable death in their transportation thither. This piratical warfare, the opprobrium of *Infidel* powers, is the warfare of the *Christian* king of Great Britain. Determined to keep open a market where *men* should be bought and sold, he has prostituted his negative for suppressing every legislative attempt to prohibit or to restrain this execrable commerce. And, that this assemblage of horrors might want no fact of distinguished die, he is now exciting those very people to rise in arms among us, and to purchase that liberty of which he has deprived them, by murdering the people on whom he also obtruded them; thus paying off former crimes committed against the *liberties* of one people with crimes which he urges them to commit against the *lives* of another." — *Jefferson's Works*, vol. i. pp. 23, 24.

John Adams, who was associated with Jefferson on the sub-committee for framing the Declaration, thus expresses his feelings on seeing Mr. Jefferson's first draught: " I was delighted with its high tone, and the flights of oratory with which it abounded, especially that concerning negro slavery; which, though I knew his Southern brethren would never suffer to pass in Congress, I certainly would never oppose." — *Works*, ii. 514.

The foresight of Mr. Adams, concerning the rejection of the passage relating to slavery, was not founded on a belief that the sentiments contained in it were at variance with the general views of the people both at the South and at the North (for the history of the times is full of evidence to the contrary), but from his knowledge that a few bold and persevering pro-slavery men would be able then — as they have been ever since — to induce timid and time-serving, and even honest but less strong-willed, public servants, to concede to them, for the sake of peace and harmony, all they demanded.

Lord Mahon asserts that the rejected clause, " it was found, would displease the Southern Colonies, who had never sought to prohibit the importation of slaves, but, on the contrary, desired to continue it." *Lord Mahon's error.*

Our worthy Corresponding Member, the Hon. Peter Force, of Washington, (in two communications to the " National Intelligencer," January 16th and 18th, 1855, — republished in London in the form of a pamphlet,) has completely refuted this error ; and has produced abundant evidence that the " Southern Colonies, jointly with all the others, and separately each for itself, did agree to prohibit the importation of slaves, voluntarily and in good faith." He calls attention to the Continental Association, adopted and signed by all the members of the Congress on the 20th of October, 1774.

" The second Article of the Association is in these words : —

" ' That we will neither import nor purchase any slave imported after the first day of December next ; after which we will wholly discontinue the slave-trade, and will neither be concerned in it ourselves, nor will we hire our vessels nor sell our commodities or manufactures to those who are concerned in it.' *Continental Association.*

" This was signed by all the Delegates of the twelve Colonies represented in it. . . .

"As Georgia was not represented in the Congress of 1774, the Association could have no signatures from that Colony. But the people of Georgia, as soon as they could speak by their Representatives, expressed themselves as distinctly on this point as any of their brethren of the Southern Colonies. The following are among the resolutions adopted by the Provincial Congress of Georgia, on Thursday, July 6th, 1775:—

Provincial Congress of Georgia. "'1. *Resolved*, That this Congress will adopt, and carry into execution, all and singular the measures and recommendations of the late Continental Congress.

"'4. *Resolved*, That we will neither import or purchase any slave imported from Africa or elsewhere after this day.'

"The Continental Association was also adopted by the Maryland Convention on the 8th of December, 1774; by the South-Carolina Provincial Congress on the 11th of January, 1775; by the Virginia Convention on the 22d of March, 1775; and by the North-Carolina Provincial Congress on the 23d of August, 1775. The Assembly of Delaware, on the 25th of March, 1775, passed a bill to prohibit the importation of slaves into that Government; but this was returned by the governor, John Penn, who refused to give it his assent.

"Thus the Southern Colonies, as far as was possible, besides giving their assent to the Association of the Congress by the signatures of their delegates to that compact, each, in their several Congresses and Conventions, separately expressed their approval of it, and their determination to support it."

The articles of the Continental Association were not allowed to remain a dead letter. The enforcement of the rules was intrusted to committees in the several Colonies. The action of one of these committees, in the case of the violation of the second article by Mr. John Brown, a merchant of Norfolk, in Virginia, is seen in the following address:—

" ' TO THE FREEMEN OF VIRGINIA :

" ' COMMITTEE CHAMBER, NORFOLK, March 6, 1775.

" ' Trusting to your sure resentment against the enemies of your *Continental Associa-* country, we, the committee, elected by ballot for the Borough of Nor- *tion.* folk, hold up for your just indignation Mr. John Brown, merchant of this place.

" ' On Thursday, the 2d of March, this committee were informed of the arrival of the brig Fanny, Capt. Watson, with a number of slaves for Mr. Brown; and, upon inquiry, it appeared they were shipped from Jamaica as his property, and on his account; that he had taken great pains to conceal their arrival from the knowledge of the committee; and that the shipper of the slaves, Mr. Brown's correspondent, and the captain of the vessel, were all fully apprised of the Continental prohibition against that article.

" ' From the whole of this transaction, therefore, we, the committee for Norfolk Borough, do give it as our unanimous opinion, that the said John Brown has wilfully and perversely violated the Continental Association to which he had with his own hand subscribed obedience; and that, agreeable to the eleventh article, we are bound forthwith to publish the truth of the case, to the end that all such foes to the rights of British America may be publicly known and universally contemned as the enemies of American liberty, and that every person may henceforth break off all dealings with him.'

" This decision of the Norfolk Committee," continues Mr. Force, " on the importation of the slaves by Mr. Brown, in violation of the Continental Association, told the whole story as to who were, and who were not, in favor of continuing it. The importers of the negroes were the supporters of the Crown; the importation was opposed by the friends of the Colonies." — *Notes on Lord Mahon's History of the American Declaration of Independence*, pp. 43-46.

Lord Mahon's error arose from applying to " the Southern *Lord Mahon's* Colonies " in general the remarks of Mr. Jefferson (" Writ- *error.* ings," vol. i. p. 19) relating to the delegates from South Carolina and Georgia. In the same passage in which these Colonies are mentioned with discredit, the pro-slavery men at the North, whose mercenary spirit was to be met, are equally censured. Still, there cannot be any doubt that the prevailing sentiment of the *people* at the South, as well as at the North, was decidedly opposed to slavery. The evil was almost universally regarded as temporary, and no one openly advocated its perpetuation.

Before passing from the consideration of the Declaration of Independence, let us look, for a moment, at the practical interpretation of its language, as furnished by the early legislation of some of the States.

The declaration that all men are born equal, and that they possess the unalienable right of *liberty*, was re-affirmed by several of the States, and adopted as a part of their Constitutions. The action of our own Commonwealth, in this respect, was clearly shown by the Rev. Dr. Belknap, the founder of our Society, in his " Answers to Queries respecting Slavery," proposed to him by the Hon. Judge Tucker of Virginia, January 24th, 1795.

Rev. Dr.
Belknap.

" The present Constitution of Massachusetts was established in 1780. The first article of the Declaration of Rights asserts that ' all men are born free and equal.' This was inserted not merely as a moral or political truth, but with a particular view to establish the liberation of the negroes on a general principle ; and so it was understood by the people at large ; but some doubted whether this were sufficient.

" Many of the blacks, taking advantage of the *public opinion* and of this general assertion in the Bill of Rights, asked their freedom, and obtained it. Others took it without leave. Some of the aged and infirm thought it most prudent to continue in the families where they had always been well used, and experience has proved that they acted right.

" In 1781, at the Court in Worcester County, an indictment was found against a white man for assaulting, beating, and imprisoning a black. He was tried at the Supreme Judicial Court in 1783. His defence was, that the black was his slave ; and that the beating, &c. was the necessary restraint and correction of the master. This was answered by citing the aforesaid clause in the Declaration of Rights. The judges and jury were of opinion, that he had no right to beat or imprison the negro. He was found guilty, and fined forty shillings. This decision was a mortal wound to slavery in Massachusetts." — *Mass. Hist. Coll.*, First Series, vol. iv. p. 203.

The Hon. Emory Washburn, in his admirable paper on the "Extinction of Slavery in Massachusetts," communicated to our Society at the regular meeting in May, 1857, and published in the Proceedings for that year, gives a pretty full account of this trial.

The brief used by Mr. Lincoln, the counsel for the negro, was placed in the hands of Mr. Washburn by the son of the eminent counsellor, our venerable and respected associate, the Hon. Levi Lincoln of Worcester, for many years Governor of this Commonwealth. Every word of it, and of the whole paper of Mr. Washburn, ought to be carefully read and pondered at the present time. A few extracts will give some idea of the character of the arguments so effectively used at that period, when the authors of the Declaration of Independence and the founders of the Republic were still struggling to establish our Government on the firm basis of equal and eternal justice. A solemn appeal to the "*higher law*" was not, in those days, denounced as moral or political heresy. *Brief of Mr. Lincoln.*

" When a fellow-subject is restrained of his liberty, it is an attack upon every other subject; and every one has a right to aid him in regaining his liberty.

" What, in this respect, are to be the consequences of your verdict ? Will it not be tidings of great joy to this community ? It is virtually opening the prison-doors, and letting the oppressed go free !

" Could they expect to triumph in their struggle with Great Britain, and become free themselves, until they let those go free who were under them ? Were they not acting like Pharaoh and the Egyptians, if they refused to set these free ?

" But the plaintiff insists that it is not true, as stated in the Constitution, that all men are born free; for children are born and placed under the power and control of their parents.

" This may be. But they are not born as slaves: they are under

the power of their parents, to be nursed and nurtured and educated for
their good.

"And the black child is born as much a free child in this sense as
if it were white.

.   .   .   .   .

"In making out that negroes are the property of their masters,
the counsel for the plaintiff speak of lineage, and contend that the
children of slaves must be slaves in the same way that, because our
first parents fell, we all fell with them.

"But are not all mankind born in the same way? Are not their
bodies clothed with the same kind of flesh? Was not the same breath
of life breathed into all? We are under the same gospel dispensation,
have one common Saviour, inhabit the same globe, die in the same
manner; and though the white man may have his body wrapped in
fine linen, and his attire may be a little more decorated, there all distinction of man's making ends. We all sleep on the same level in the
dust. We shall all be raised by the sound of one common trump,
calling unto all that are in their graves, without distinction, to arise;
shall be arraigned at one common bar; shall have one common Judge,
and be tried by one common jury, and condemned or acquitted by one
common law, — by the gospel, the perfect law of liberty.

"This cause will then be tried again, and your verdict will there
be tried. Therefore, gentlemen of the jury, let me conjure you to
give such a verdict now as will stand this test, and be approved by
your own minds in the last moments of your existence, and by your
Judge at the last day.

"It will then be tried by the laws of reason and revelation.

"Is it not a law of nature, that all men are equal and free?

"Is not the law of nature the law of God?

"Is not the law of God, then, against slavery?

"If there is no law of man establishing it, there is no difficulty.
If there is, then the great difficulty is to determine which law you
ought to obey; and, if you shall have the same ideas as I have of
present and future things, you will obey the former.

"The worst that can happen to you for disobeying the former is
the destruction of the body; for the last, that of your souls." — *Proceedings of the Mass. Hist. Soc.*, 1855–58, pp. 198–201.

Other contemporary documents might be cited to show
how such language as that used in the Declaration of Inde-

pendence was interpreted by the legislative and legal action of the day. I will only give the first article in the Constitution of Vermont: —

" All men are born equally free and independent, and have certain natural, inherent, and inalienable rights ; among which are the enjoying and defending life and liberty ; acquiring, possessing, and protecting property ; and pursuing and obtaining happiness and safety : *therefore* no male person, born in this country or brought from over sea, ought to be holden by law to serve any person as a servant, slave, or apprentice, after he arrives to the age of twenty-one years ; nor female, in like manner, after she arrives to the age of eighteen years ; unless they are bound by their own consent after they arrive to such age, or bound by the law for the payment of debts, damages, fines, costs, or the like." *Constitution of Vermont.*

The articles of Confederation — which constituted the Law of the Land from the time of their passage in 1778 to the adoption of the Federal Constitution — recognized and granted to free negroes the same privileges of citizenship which belonged to white inhabitants. The fourth article is as follows : — *Articles of Confederation.*

" ART. 4. — The better to secure and perpetuate mutual friendship and intercourse among the people of the different States in this Union, the free inhabitants of each of these States — paupers, vagabonds, and fugitives from justice excepted — shall be entitled to all privileges and immunities of free citizens in the several States ; and the people of each State shall have free ingress and regress to and from any other State, and shall enjoy therein all the privileges of trade and commerce, subject to the same duties, impositions, and restrictions as the inhabitants thereof, respectively ; provided that such restrictions shall not extend so far as to prevent the removal of property imported into any State from any other State, of which the owner is an inhabitant ; provided, also, that no imposition, duty, or restriction, shall be laid by any State on the property of the United States, or either of them." — *Elliot's Debates*, vol. i. p. 79. *Free negroes regarded as citizens.*

It was not by accident or oversight that negroes were included in the phrase " free inhabitants " ; for, when this article was under consideration, the delegates from South Carolina moved to amend, by inserting between the words "free" and "inhabitants" the word "*white*." The proposed amendment was lost; *only two* States voting in the affirmative.

In the ninth article, the word "white" was retained. The State of New Jersey, although a slaveholding State, objected to this, and made a representation to Congress on the subject; an extract from which is pertinent here : —

New Jersey objects to the omission of negroes.
"The ninth article also provides that the requisition for the land forces, to be furnished by the several States, shall be proportioned to the number of *white* inhabitants in each. In the act of Independence, we find the following declaration : 'We hold these truths to be self-evident : that all men are created equal ; that they are endued by their Creator with certain unalienable rights, among which are life, liberty, and the pursuit of happiness.' Of this doctrine it is not a very remote consequence, that all the inhabitants of every society, be the color of their complexion what it may, are bound to promote the interest thereof, according to their respective abilities. They ought, therefore, to be brought into the account, on this occasion. But admitting necessity or expediency to justify the refusal of liberty, in certain circumstances, to persons of a particular color, we think it unequal to reckon upon such in this case. Should it be improper, for special local reasons, to admit them in arms for the defence of the nation, yet we conceive the proportion of forces to be embodied ought to be fixed according to the whole number of inhabitants in the State, from whatever class they may be raised. If the whole number of inhabitants in a State, whose inhabitants are all whites, both those who are called into the field and those who remain to till the ground and labor in mechanical arts and otherwise, are reckoned in the estimate for striking the proportion of forces to be furnished by that State, ought even a part of the latter description to be left out in another ? As it is of indispensable necessity, in every war, that a part of the inhabitants be employed for the uses of husbandry and otherwise at home, while others are called into the field, there must be the same propriety that owners of a different color, who are employed for this purpose in one State, while *whites* are employed for the same purpose in another, be reckoned in the account of the inhabitants in the present instance." — *Elliot's Debates*, vol. i. p. 89.

The opinions of the founders of the Republic respecting Opinions of the Founders of the Re-public. the slavery and the citizenship of negroes, as expressed in some of the most important of their public acts, from the commencement to the close of their struggle for National Independence, and during the period of the Confederation, may be gathered from the documents already cited. They had proclaimed to the world the Universal Magna Charta which the Creator and Governor of men had granted to his subjects. This charter of natural and unalienable rights had been timidly read and faintly spoken, by now and then a friend of liberty, in earlier times. Our patriot Fathers were the first boldly to publish it to "mankind"; to adopt these "self-evident truths" as their National Creed; and, "appealing to the Supreme Judge of the universe for the rectitude of their intentions," to announce their solemn purpose of establishing a Government, with these principles for its chief cornerstone.

With such principles and motives to stimulate their patriotism and nerve their courage, they could not fail. The mighty power of the mother-country was impotent when wielded against the cause of Liberty. The Independence of the United States was acknowledged by Great Britain, and we took our place among the nations of the earth.

The Articles of Confederation served their purpose during the war, but were found inadequate to the growing wants of the Government. A Convention was accordingly called, to meet in Philadelphia on the second Monday in May in 1787, to frame a Constitution.

Before considering particularly the language of the *Constitution*, "the palladium of our liberties," let us look for a moment at some of the men to whom was intrusted this important work, and see with what minds they came to the performance of the duty assigned them.

Among the delegates, we find the names of George Washington of Virginia, and Benjamin Franklin of Pennsylvania.

The former was unanimously elected President of the Convention.   Dr. Franklin was the only man who could have been
thought of as a competitor for the place.   He was to have
made the nomination of Washington : but, owing to the state
of the weather and of his health, he was confined to his
house ; and his colleague, Robert Morris, in behalf of the delegation from Pennsylvania, proposed " George Washington, Esq.,
late Commander-in-chief," for President of the Convention.

The character and position of these two pre-eminent patriots, from different States, one a slave-holder and the other
not, give the greatest weight to their opinions.   They have
both left distinct records of their views on the subject of
slavery.

Though, by inheritance and other circumstances entirely
beyond his control, Washington found himself a slave-holder,
yet he never defended the institution of slavery, or desired
its perpetuity.   On the contrary, we find, that, before he had
drawn his sword in defence of the independence of his country, he had uttered his testimony against slavery in the fullest
manner ;. and, through his whole life, his desire to clear himself and his country from the foul blot was sincere and
constant.

It had become quite common, during the year preceding
the commencement of hostilities between the colonists and
the mother-country, for the people to meet in their respective
counties or towns, to express, through addresses and resolutions, their sentiments and views respecting the condition of
affairs.   Such a meeting was held on the 18th of July, 1774,
at the Fairfax County Court House, in Virginia ; and a series
of twenty-four resolutions, prepared by a Committee of which
Washington was chairman, was adopted.

Three of these resolutions are here given : —

" 17. *Resolved*, That it is the opinion of this meeting, that, during
our present difficulties and distress, no slaves ought to be imported
into any of the British colonies on this continent ; and we take this

opportunity of declaring our most earnest wishes to see an entire stop for ever put to such a wicked, cruel, and unnatural trade. . . .

"21. *Resolved*, That it is the opinion of this meeting, that this and the other associating colonies should break off all trade, intercourse, and dealings with that colony, province, or town, which shall decline, or refuse to agree to, the plan which shall be adopted by the General Congress. . . . . .

"24. *Resolved*, That George Washington and Charles Broadwater, lately elected our representatives to serve in the General Assembly, be appointed to attend the Convention at Williamsburg on the first day of August next, and present these resolves, as the sense of the people of this county upon the measures proper to be taken in the present alarming and dangerous situation of America."

Respecting these resolutions, Mr. Sparks observes : —

"The draught, from which the resolves are printed, I find among Washington's papers, in the handwriting of George Mason, by whom they were probably drawn up ; yet, as they were adopted by the Committee of which Washington was chairman, and reported by him as moderator of the meeting, they may be presumed to express his opinions, formed on a perfect knowledge of the subject, and after cool deliberation. This may indeed be inferred from his letter to Mr. Bryan Fairfax, in which he intimates a doubt only as to the article favoring the idea of a further petition to the king. He was opposed to such a step, believing enough had been done in this way already ; but he yielded the point in tenderness to the more wavering resolution of his associates.

"These resolves are framed with much care and ability, and exhibit the question then at issue, and the state of public feeling, in a manner so clear and forcible as to give them a special claim to a place in the present work, in addition to the circumstance of their being the matured views of Washington at the outset of the great Revolutionary struggle in which he was to act so conspicuous a part. . . .

"Such were the opinions of Washington, and his associates in Virginia, at the beginning of the Revolutionary contest. The seventeenth resolve merits attention, from the pointed manner in which it condemns the slave-trade." — *Sparks's Washington*, vol. ii. pp. 488, 494, 495.

Washington not only condemned the slave-trade, but expressed in the most decided terms his disapprobation of
domestic slavery. He discountenanced the interference of
non-slaveholders in attempting to liberate slaves without the
consent of their masters; but at the same time, in a letter
on the subject to Robert Morris, 12th April, 1786, he was
careful to add: —

" I hope it will not be conceived from these observations that it is
my wish to hold the unhappy people, who are the subject of this letter,
in slavery. I can only say, that there is not a man living who wishes
more sincerely than I do to see some plan adopted for the abolition of
it : but there is only one proper and effectual mode by which this can
be accomplished, and that is by legislative authority ; and this, as far
as my suffrage will go, shall never be wanting." — *Sparks's Washington*, vol. ix. p. 159.

On the 9th of September of this same year, Washington
wrote to Mr. John F. Mercer, of Maryland: —

" I never mean, unless some particular circumstance should compel
me to it, to possess another slave by purchase ; it being among my
first wishes to see some plan adopted by which slavery in this country
may be abolished by law." — *Ibid.*

That Washington believed his wishes with regard to the
abolition of slavery would at no distant day be realized, is
evident from a letter to Sir John Sinclair, 11th December,
1796: —

" The present prices of lands in Pennsylvania are higher than they
are in Maryland and Virginia, although they are not of superior quality ; [among other reasons] because there are laws here for the gradual
abolition of slavery, which neither of the two States above mentioned
have at present, but which nothing is more certain than they must
have, and at a period not remote." — *Sparks's Washington*, vol. xii.
p. 326.

Lafayette, the bosom friend, who shared so fully the confidence and sympathy of Washington, was in frequent correspondence with him on the subject of slavery.

No sooner had hostilities ceased, than he set about devising some practical plan for ridding the country, which his valor had helped to free from the yoke of British oppression, of an evil which he declared to be "a crime much blacker than any African face."

On the 5th of February, 1783, Lafayette writes: —

"Now, my dear General, that you are going to enjoy some ease Lafayette. and quiet, permit me to propose a plan to you, which might become greatly beneficial to the black part of mankind. Let us unite in purchasing a small estate, where we may try the experiment to free the negroes, and use them only as tenants. Such an example as yours might render it a general practice ; and, if we succeed in America, I will cheerfully devote a part of my time to render the method fashionable in the West Indies. If it be a wild scheme, I had rather be mad in this way, than to be thought wise in the other task." — *Correspondence of the American Revolution*, vol. iii. p. 547.

To this letter Washington replies, April 5th, 1783 : —

"The scheme, my dear Marquis, which you propose as a precedent Washington. to encourage the emancipation of the black people in this country from that state of bondage in which they are held, is a striking evidence of the benevolence of your heart. I shall be happy to join you in so laudable a work, but will defer going into a detail of the business till I have the pleasure of seeing you." — *Sparks's Washington*, vol. viii. pp. 414, 415.

Three years later, and after Lafayette had put his plan into practice, Washington wrote to him in a tone of mingled approval of what he had done, and despondency as to any immediate action on the subject in this country : —

"MOUNT VERNON, 10th May, 1786.

"The benevolence of your heart, my dear Marquis, is so conspicuous upon all occasions, that I never wonder at any fresh proofs of it ; but your late purchase of an estate in the colony of Cayenne, with a view of emancipating the slaves on it, is a generous and noble proof of your humanity. Would to God a like spirit might diffuse itself generally into the minds of the people of this country ! But I despair

Washington.

of seeing it. Some petitions were presented to the Assembly, at its last session, for the abolition of slavery; but they could scarcely obtain a reading. To set the slaves afloat at once, would, I really believe, be productive of much inconvenience and mischief; but by degrees it certainly might, and assuredly ought to be effected, and that, too, by legislative authority." — *Sparks's Washington*, vol. ix. pp. 163, 164.

The following note on this subject is added by Mr. Sparks:

Lafayette.

" In a remarkable and very interesting letter, written by Lafayette in the prison of Magdeburg [March 15, 1793, to the Princess d'Hénin], he said, ' I know not what disposition has been made of my plantation at Cayenne; but I hope Madame de Lafayette will take care that the negroes, who cultivate it, shall preserve their liberty.' "

To John Adams, also, Lafayette wrote from Paris in 1786:

" In the cause of my black brethren, I feel myself warmly interested, and most decidedly side, so far as respects them, against the white part of mankind. Whatever be the complexion of the enslaved, it does not, in my opinion, alter the complexion of the crime which the enslaver commits, — a crime much blacker than any African face. It is to me a matter of great anxiety and concern, to find that this trade is sometimes perpetrated under the flag of liberty, our dear and noble stripes, to which virtue and glory have been constant standard-bearers." — *Life and Works of John Adams*, vol. viii. p. 376.

The opinions with regard to slavery which Washington held before the adoption of the Federal Constitution were never relinquished. Only two years before he died (as we learn from Mr. Irving, who had the original letter before him), he said, writing to his nephew, Lawrence Lewis, " I wish from my soul that the Legislature of this State could see the policy of a gradual abolition of slavery. It might prevent much future mischief."

Washington's Will.

" On opening the will which he had handed to Mrs. Washington shortly before his death, it was found to have been carefully drawn up by himself in the preceding July; and, *by an act in conformity with his whole career*, one of its first provisions directed the emancipation of his slaves on the decease of his wife. It had long been his earnest wish, that the slaves held by him *in his own right* should receive their freedom during his life; but he had found that it would be attended with insuperable difficulties, on account of their intermixture by marriage with the 'dower negroes,' whom it was not in his power to manumit under the tenure by which they were held.

"With provident benignity, he also made provision in his will for such as were to receive their freedom under this devise, but who, from age, bodily infirmities, or infancy, might be unable to support themselves; and he expressly forbade, under any pretence whatsoever, the sale or transportation out of Virginia, of any slave of whom he might die possessed. Though born and educated a slave-holder, this was all in consonance with feelings, sentiments, and principles which he had long entertained." — *Irving's Washington,* vol. v. pp. 316, 317.

The second item of that long will, coming immediately after the bequest to his "dearly beloved wife," is here given: —

"*Item.* — Upon the decease of my wife, it is my will and desire that all slaves whom I hold *in my own right* shall receive their freedom. To emancipate them during her life, would, though earnestly wished by me, be attended with such insuperable difficulties, on account of their intermixture by marriage with the dower negroes, as to excite the most painful sensations, if not disagreeable consequences to the latter, while both descriptions are in the occupancy of the same proprietor; it not being in my power, under the tenure by which the dower negroes are held, to manumit them. And whereas, among those who will receive freedom according to this devise, there may be some, who, from old age or bodily infirmities, and others, who, on account of their infancy, will be unable to support themselves, it is my will and desire, that all who come under the first and second description shall be comfortably clothed and fed by my heirs while they live; and that such of the latter description as have no parents living, or, if living, are unable or unwilling to provide for them, shall be bound by the court until they shall arrive at the age of twenty-five years; and in cases where no record can be produced, whereby their ages can be ascertained, the judgment of the court, upon its own view of the subject, shall be adequate and final. The negroes thus bound, are (by their masters or mistresses) to be taught to read and write, and to be brought up to some useful occupation, agreeably to the laws of the Commonwealth of Virginia providing for the support of orphan and other poor children. And I do hereby expressly forbid the sale or

Washing-
ton's Will.

transportation out of the said Commonwealth, of any slave I may die possessed of, under any pretence whatsoever. And I do, moreover, most pointedly and most solemnly enjoin it upon my executors hereafter named, or the survivors of them, to see that this clause respecting slaves, and every part thereof, be religiously fulfilled at the epoch at which it is directed to take place, without evasion, neglect, or delay, after the crops which may then be on the ground are harvested, particularly as it respects the aged and infirm ; seeing that a regular and permanent fund be established for their support, as long as there are subjects requiring it ; not trusting to the uncertain provision to be made by individuals. And to my mulatto man, *William*, calling himself *William Lee*, I give immediate freedom ; or, if he should prefer it (on account of the accidents which have befallen him, and which have rendered him incapable of walking or of any active employment), to remain in the situation he now is, it shall be optional in him to do so : in either case, however, I allow him an annuity of thirty dollars, during his natural life, which shall be independent of the victuals and clothes he has been accustomed to receive, if he chooses the last alternative ; but in full with his freedom, if he prefers the first. And this I give him as a testimony of my sense of his attachment to me, and for his faithful services during the revolutionary war." — *Sparks's Washington*, vol. xii. pp. 569–570.

Franklin.

Franklin's opinions on the subject of slavery agreed substantially with those entertained by Washington; and, like "the Father of his Country," this great philosopher, patriot, and statesman not only denounced negro slavery when struggling for national liberty, but left, among his last legacies to his countrymen, the most emphatic testimony against the institution.

In a letter to John Wright of London, he gives an account of the early endeavors of the Friends in this country to abolish slavery; and, at the same time, expresses incidentally his own views on the subject : —

Early
efforts
against
slavery.

" I wish success to your endeavors for obtaining an abolition of the slave-trade. The epistle from your Yearly Meeting, for the year 1758, was not the *first sowing* of the good seed you mention ; for I find, by an old pamphlet in my possession, that George Keith, near a hundred years since, wrote a paper against the practice, said to be *Early* 'given forth by the appointment of the meeting held by him at Philip *efforts against* James's house, in the city of Philadelphia, about the year 1693'; *slavery.* wherein a strict charge was given to Friends, 'that they should set their negroes at liberty, after some reasonable time of service, &c. &c.' And, about the year 1728 or 1729, I myself printed a book for Ralph Sandyford, another of your Friends in this city, against keeping negroes in slavery; two editions of which he distributed gratis. And, about the year 1736, I printed another book on the same subject, for Benjamin Lay, who also professed being one of your Friends; and he distributed the books chiefly among them. By these instances, it appears that the seed was indeed sown in the good ground of your profession, though much earlier than the time you mention; and its springing up to effect at last, though so late, is some confirmation of Lord Bacon's observation, that *a good motion never dies;* and it may encourage us in making such, though hopeless of their taking immediate effect." — *Sparks's Franklin*, vol. x. p. 403.

In a letter to Dean Woodward, dated London, April 10th, 1773, Dr. Franklin says, —

. . . "I have since had the satisfaction to learn that a disposition *Franklin.* to abolish slavery prevails in North America; that many of the Pennsylvanians have set their slaves at liberty; and that even the Virginia Assembly have petitioned the king for permission to make a law for preventing the importation of more into that Colony. This request, however, will probably not be granted, as their former laws of that kind have always been repealed, and as the interest of a few merchants here has more weight with Government than that of thousands at a distance." — *Sparks's Franklin*, vol. viii. p. 42.

In 1789 was issued an address to the public, bearing the signature of this venerable man, then in his eighty-fourth year, the last of his life. This address is here reprinted entire : —

"AN ADDRESS TO THE PUBLIC.

"*From the Pennsylvania Society for Promoting the Abolition of Slavery, and the Relief of Free Negroes unlawfully held in Bondage.*

"It is with peculiar satisfaction we assure the friends of humanity, that, in prosecuting the design of our association, our endeavors have proved successful, far beyond our most sanguine expectations.

"Encouraged by this success, and by the daily progress of that luminous and benign spirit of liberty which is diffusing itself throughout the world, and humbly hoping for the continuance of the divine blessing on our labors, we have ventured to make an important addition to our original plan; and do therefore earnestly solicit the support and assistance of all who can feel the tender emotions of sympathy and compassion, or relish the exalted pleasure of beneficence.

"Slavery is such an atrocious debasement of human nature, that its very extirpation, if not performed with solicitous care, may sometimes open a source of serious evils.

"The unhappy man, who has long been treated as a brute animal, too frequently sinks beneath the common standard of the human species. The galling chains that bind his body do also fetter his intellectual faculties, and impair the social affections of his heart. Accustomed to move like a mere machine, by the will of a master, reflection is suspended; he has not the power of choice; and reason and conscience have but little influence over his conduct, because he is chiefly governed by the passion of fear. He is poor and friendless; perhaps worn out by extreme labor, age, and disease.

"Under such circumstances, freedom may often prove a misfortune to himself, and prejudicial to society.

"Attention to emancipated black people, it is therefore to be hoped, will become a branch of our national police; but, as far as we contribute to promote this emancipation, so far that attention is evidently a serious duty incumbent on us, and which we mean to discharge to the best of our judgment and abilities.

"To instruct, to advise, to qualify those who have been restored to freedom, for the exercise and enjoyment of civil liberty; to promote in them habits of industry; to furnish them with employments suited to their age, sex, talents, and other circumstances; and to procure their children an education calculated for their future situation in life, — these are the great outlines of the annexed plan, which we have adopted, and which we conceive will essentially promote the public good, and the happiness of these our hitherto too much neglected fellow-creatures.

"A plan so extensive cannot be carried into execution without considerable pecuniary resources, beyond the present ordinary funds of the Society. We hope much from the generosity of enlightened and benevolent freemen, and will gratefully receive any donations or

subscriptions for this purpose which may be made to our Treasurer, Franklin.
James Starr, or to James Pemberton, Chairman of our Committee of
Correspondence.   " Signed by order of the Society,

"B. FRANKLIN, *President.*

"PHILADELPHIA, 9th of November, 1789."

The last public act of Dr. Franklin was the signing, as
President of the Pennsylvania Abolition Society, of the following memorial to Congress:—

" The memorial respectfully showeth,—

" That, from a regard for the happiness of mankind, an associa- Memorial to Con-
tion was formed several years since in this State, by a number of her gress, 1790.
citizens, of various religious denominations, for promoting the abolition of slavery, and for the relief of those unlawfully held in bondage.
A just and acute conception of the true principles of liberty, as it
spread through the land, produced accessions to their numbers, many
friends to their cause, and a legislative co-operation with their views,
which, by the blessing of Divine Providence, have been successfully
directed to the relieving from bondage a large number of their fellow-
creatures of the African race. They have also the satisfaction to
observe, that, in consequence of that spirit of philanthropy and genu-
ine liberty which is generally diffusing its beneficial influence, similar
institutions are forming at home and abroad.

" That mankind are all formed by the same Almighty Being, alike
objects of his care, and equally designed for the enjoyment of happiness, the Christian religion teaches us to believe, and the political
creed of Americans fully coincides with the position. Your memorialists, particularly engaged in attending to the distresses arising from
slavery, believe it their indispensable duty to present this subject to
your notice. They have observed, with real satisfaction, that many
important and salutary powers are vested in you for ' promoting
the welfare and securing the blessings of liberty to the people of the
United States'; and as they conceive that these blessings ought right-
fully to be administered, without distinction of color, to all descriptions
of people, so they indulge themselves in the pleasing expectation, that
nothing which can be done for the relief of the unhappy objects of
their care, will be either omitted or delayed.

" From a persuasion that equal liberty was originally the portion,
and is still the birth-right, of all men ; and influenced by the strong

Franklin. ties of humanity, and the principles of their institution, your memorialists conceive themselves bound to use all justifiable endeavors to loosen the bands of slavery, and promote a general enjoyment of the blessings of freedom.   Under these impressions, they earnestly entreat your serious attention to the subject of slavery; that you will be pleased to countenance the restoration of liberty to those unhappy men, who alone, in this land of freedom, are degraded into perpetual bondage, and who, amidst the general joy of surrounding freemen, are groaning in servile subjection; that you will devise means for removing this inconsistency from the character of the American people; that you will promote mercy and justice towards this distressed race; and that you will step to the very verge of the power vested in you for discouraging every species of traffic in the persons of our fellow-men.

" Benj. Franklin, President.

" Philadelphia, February 3, 1790."

(Annals of Congress, vol. ii. p. 1197.)

The memorial occasioned a debate, in which some of the members attempted to justify slavery. This gave rise to a characteristic paper, communicated by Dr. Franklin to the " Federal Gazette " of March 25, 1790, and dated only twenty-four days before his death. By way of parody, he exposes the absurdity of the reasoning adopted by those who opposed the memorial: —

" To the Editor of the 'Federal Gazette.'

" March 23, 1790.

" Sir, — Reading last night in your excellent paper the speech of Mr. Jackson in Congress against their meddling with the affair of slavery, or attempting to mend the condition of the slaves, it put me in mind of a similar one, made about one hundred years since, by Sidi Mehemet Ibrahim, a member of the Divan of Algiers, which may be seen in Martin's Account of his Consulship, anno 1687. It was against granting the petition of the sect called *Erika*, or Purists, who prayed for the abolition of piracy and slavery as being unjust. Mr. Jackson does not quote it: perhaps he has not seen it. If, therefore, some of its reasonings are to be found in his eloquent speech, it may only show that men's interests and intellects operate, and are operated on, with surprising similarity in all countries and climates, whenever they are under similar circumstances. The African's speech, as translated, is as follows: —

" '*Allah Bismillah, &c. God is great, and Mahomet is his Prophet.*

" ' Have these Erika considered the consequences of granting their petition ? If we cease our cruises against the Christians, how shall we be furnished with the commodities their countries produce, and which are so necessary for us ? If we forbear to make slaves of their people, who, in this hot climate, are to cultivate our lands ? Who are to perform the common labors of our city, and in our families ? Must we not then be our own slaves ? And is there not more compassion and more favor due to us as Mussulmen than to these Christian dogs ? We have now above fifty thousand slaves in and near Algiers. This number, if not kept up by fresh supplies, will soon diminish, and be gradually annihilated. If we, then, cease taking and plundering the infidel ships, making slaves of the seamen and passengers. our lands will become of no value for want of cultivation ; the rents of houses in the city will sink one-half; and the revenue of government, arising from its share of prizes, be totally destroyed. And for what ? To gratify the whims of a whimsical sect, who would have us not only forbear making more slaves, but even manumit those we have.

" ' But who is to indemnify their masters for the loss ? Will the State do it ? Is our treasury sufficient ? Will the Erika do it ? Can they do it ? Or would they, to do what they think justice to the slaves, do a greater injustice to the owners ? And, if we set our slaves free, what is to be done with them ? Few of them will return to their countries ; they know too well the greater hardships they must there be subject to ; they will not embrace our holy religion ; they will not adopt our manners; our people will not pollute themselves by inter-marrying with them. Must we maintain them as beggars in our streets, or suffer our properties to be the prey of their pillage ? For men accustomed to slavery will not work for a livelihood when not compelled. And what is there so pitiable in their present condition ? Were they not slaves in their own countries ?

" ' Are not Spain, Portugal, France. and the Italian States, governed by despots, who hold all their subjects in slavery, without exception ? Even England treats its sailors as slaves : for they are, whenever the government pleases, seized, and confined in ships of war ; condemned not only to work, but to fight, for small wages, or a mere subsistence, not better than our slaves are allowed by us. Is their condition, then, made worse by their falling into our hands ? No: they have only exchanged one slavery for another, and I may say, a better; for here they are brought into a land where the sun of Islamism gives forth its light, and shines in full splendor; and they have an opportunity of making themselves acquainted with the true doctrine, and thereby saving their immortal souls. Those who remain at home have not that happiness. Sending the slaves home, then, would be sending them out of light into darkness.

" ' I repeat the question, What is to be done with them? I have heard it suggested that they may be planted in the wilderness, where there is plenty of land for them to subsist on, and where they may flourish as a free State; but they are, I doubt, too little disposed to labor without compulsion, as well as too ignorant to establish a good government, and the wild Arabs would soon molest and destroy or again enslave them. While serving us, we take care to provide them with every thing, and they are treated with humanity. The laborers in their own country are, as I am well informed, worse fed, lodged, and clothed.

" ' The condition of most of them is, therefore, already mended, and requires no further improvement. Here their lives are in safety. They are not liable to be impressed for soldiers, and forced to cut one another's Christian throats, as in the wars of their own countries. If some of the religious mad bigots, who now tease us with their silly petitions, have, in a fit of blind zeal, freed their slaves, it was not generosity, it was not humanity, that moved them to the action: it was from the conscious burthen of a load of sins, and a hope, from the supposed merits of so good a work, to be excused from damnation.

" ' How grossly are they mistaken to suppose slavery to be disallowed by the Alcoran! Are not the two precepts, to quote no more, ' Masters, treat your slaves with kindness; slaves, serve your masters with cheerfulness and fidelity,' clear proofs to the contrary? Nor can the plundering of infidels be in that sacred book forbidden, since it is well known from it that God has given the world, and all that it contains, to his faithful Mussulmen, who are to enjoy it of right as fast as they conquer it. Let us, then, hear no more of this detestable proposition,—the manumission of Christian slaves; the adoption of which would, by depreciating our lands and houses, and thereby depriving so many good citizens of their properties, create universal discontent, and provoke insurrections, to the endangering of government, and producing general confusion. I have, therefore, no doubt but this wise council will prefer the comfort and happiness of a whole nation of true believers to the whim of a few Erika, and dismiss their petition.'

" The result was, as Martin tells us, that the Divan came to this resolution: ' The doctrine that plundering and enslaving the Christians is unjust, is, at best, *problematical;* but that it is the interest of this State to continue the practice, is clear: therefore let the petition be rejected.' Franklin's parody on a pro-slavery speech.

" And it was rejected accordingly.

" And since like motives are apt to produce in the minds of men like opinions and resolutions, may we not, Mr. Brown, venture to predict, from this account, that the petitions to the Parliament of England for abolishing the slave-trade, to say nothing of other Legislatures, and the debates upon them, will have a similar conclusion ? I am, sir, your constant reader and humble servant,

HISTORICUS."

(Sparks's Franklin, vol. ii. pp. 517–521.)

It is not necessary now to produce the opinions of other members of the Convention: some of them expressed their views fully during the debates, and specimens of their speeches will presently be given. But it is not out of place here to inquire whether the leading statesmen of the country at that time, who were not members of the Convention, held opinions substantially the same as those of Washington and Franklin.

John Adams and Thomas Jefferson — among the foremost men in founding the Republic — were, at the time the Convention was held, serving their country abroad; the former as ambassador to England; the latter, to France. The opinions of Mr. Adams on slavery may be briefly given in an extract from a letter written only a few years before his death: —

" I have, through my whole life, held the practice of slavery in such abhorrence, that I have never owned a negro or any other slave: John Adams. though I have lived for many years in times when the practice was not disgraceful ; when the best men in my vicinity thought it not inconsistent with their character ; and when it has cost me thousands of dollars for the labor and subsistence of free men, which I might have saved by the purchase of negroes at times when they were very cheap." — *Works of John Adams*, vol. x. p. 380.

Jefferson.   Mr. Jefferson's sentiments before and at the time of the Declaration of Independence have already been given. They were still more strongly expressed in his " Notes on Virginia," in 1782 : —

Notes on Virginia.   " The whole commerce between master and slave is a perpetual exercise of the most boisterous passions ; the most unremitting despotism on the one part, and degrading submissions ou the other. Our children see this, and learn to imitate it ; for man is an imitative animal. This quality is the germ of all education in him. From his cradle to his grave, he is learning to do what he sees others do. If a parent could find no motive, either in his philanthropy or his self-love, for restraining the intemperance of passion towards his slave, it should always be a sufficient one that his child is present. But generally it is not sufficient. The parent storms ; the child looks on, catches the lineaments of wrath, puts on the same airs in the circle of smaller slaves, gives a loose to the worst of passions ; and thus nursed, educated, and daily exercised in tyranny, cannot but be stamped by it with odious peculiarities. The man must be a prodigy who can retain his manners and morals undepraved by such circumstances. And with what execration should the statesman be loaded, who, permitting one-half the citizens thus to trample on the rights of the other, transforms those into despots, and these into enemies ; destroys the morals of the one part, and the *amor patriæ* of the other ! For, if a slave can have a country in this world, it must be any other in preference to that in which he is born to live and labor for another ; in which he must lock up the faculties of his nature, contribute as far as depends on his individual endeavors to the evanishment of the human race, or entail his own miserable condition on the endless generations proceeding from him. With the morals of the people, their industry also is destroyed. For in a warm climate, no man will labor for himself who can make another labor for him. This is so true, that, of the proprietors of slaves, a very small proportion indeed are ever seen to labor. And can the liberties of a nation be thought secure when we have removed their only firm basis, — a conviction in the minds of the people that these liberties are of the gift of God ? — that they are not to be violated but with his wrath ? Indeed I tremble for my country, when I reflect that God is just ; that his justice cannot sleep for ever ; that considering numbers, nature, and natural means only, a revolution of the wheel of fortune, an exchange of situation, is among possible events; that it may become probable by supernatural Jefferson. interference. The Almighty has no attribute which can take side with us in such a contest. But it is impossible to be temperate, and to pursue this subject through the various considerations of policy, of morals, of history natural and civil. We must be contented to hope they will force their way into every one's mind. I think a change already perceptible, since the origin of the present revolution. The spirit of the master is abating, — that of the slave rising from the dust; his condition mollifying; the way, I hope, preparing, under the auspices of Heaven, for a total emancipation; and that this is disposed, in the order of events, to be with the consent of the masters, rather than by their extirpation." — *Jefferson's Writings*, vol. viii. pp. 403, 404.

In a letter to Dr. Price, dated at London on the 7th of August, 1785, Mr. Jefferson thus tells him what will be the probable effect of his late pamphlet, in which the abolition of slavery is strenuously urged: —

"From the mouth to the head of the Chesapeake, the bulk of the people will approve it in theory, and it will find a respectable minority ready to adopt it in practice; a minority, which, for weight and worth of character, preponderates against the greater number, who have not the courage to divest their families of a property, which, however, keeps their conscience unquiet. Northward of the Chesapeake, you may find here and there an opponent to your doctrine, as you may find here and there a robber and murderer; but in no greater number. In that part of America, there being but few slaves, they can easily disencumber themselves of them; and emancipation is put into such a train, that in a few years there will be no slaves northward of Maryland. In Maryland, I do not find such a disposition to begin the redress of this enormity, as in Virginia. This is the next State to which we may turn our eyes for the interesting spectacle of justice in conflict with avarice and oppression; a conflict wherein the sacred side is gaining daily recruits, from the influx into office of young men grown, and growing up. These have sucked in the principles of liberty, as it were, with their mothers' milk; and it is to them I look with anxiety to turn the fate of this question. Be not therefore discouraged. What you have written will do a great deal of good; and, could you still trouble yourself with our welfare, no man is more able to give aid to the laboring side." — *Jefferson's Writings*, vol. i. p. 377.

Jefferson.   While Mr. Jefferson was in France, in 1786, he furnished M. Démeunier with many materials for his copious article on the United States, about to appear in the great "Encyclopédie Méthodique"; and he revised the manuscript of the whole article with great care. The following is part of a note to the author, most of which he translated into French, and incorporated in his own work, where it stands as a perpetual record of Mr. Jefferson's sentiments at that time : —

"M. de Meusnier, where he mentions that the slave-law has been passed in Virginia without the clause of emancipation, is pleased to mention, that neither Mr. Wythe nor Mr. Jefferson was present to make the proposition they had meditated : from which, people, who do not give themselves the trouble to reflect or inquire, might conclude hastily, that their absence was the cause why the proposition was not made ; and, of course, that there were not, in the Assembly, persons of virtue and firmness enough to propose the clause for emancipation. This supposition would not be true. There were persons there, who wanted neither the virtue to propose nor talents to enforce the proposition, had they seen that the disposition of the Legislature was ripe for it. These worthy characters would feel themselves wounded, degraded, and discouraged by this idea. Mr. Jefferson would therefore be obliged to M. de Meusnier to mention it in some such manner as this : ' Of the two commissioners, who had concerted the amendatory clause for the gradual emancipation of slaves, Mr. Wythe could not be present, he being a member of the judiciary department ; and Mr. Jefferson was absent on the legation to France. But there were not wanting, in that Assembly, men of virtue enough to propose, and talents to vindicate, this clause. But they saw that the moment of doing it with success was not yet arrived, and that an unsuccessful effort, as too often happens, would only rivet still closer the chains of bondage, and retard the moment of delivery to this oppressed description of men. What a stupendous, what an incomprehensible machine is man, who can endure toil, famine, stripes, imprisonment, and death itself, in vindication of his own liberty, and, the next moment, be deaf to all those motives whose power supported him through his trial, and inflict on his fellow-men a bondage, one hour of which is fraught with more misery than ages of that which he rose in rebellion to oppose ! But we must await with patience the workings of an overruling Providence, and hope that that is preparing the deliverance of these our Jefferson. suffering brethren. When the measure of their tears shall be full; when their groans shall have involved heaven itself in darkness, — doubtless a God of justice will awaken to their distress, and, by diffus- ing light and liberality among their oppressors, or, at length, by his exterminating thunder, manifest his attention to the things of this world, and that they are not left to the guidance of a blind fatality.' " — *Jefferson's Writings*, vol. ix. pp. 278, 279

In his " Autobiography," written only a few years before his death, alluding to the above-mentioned slave-law, he says, —

" The bill on the subject of slaves was a mere digest of the exist- ing laws respecting them, without any intimation of a plan for a future and general emancipation. It was thought better that this should be kept back, and attempted only by way of amendment, when- ever the bill should be brought on. The principles of the amendment, however, were agreed on; that is to say, the freedom of all born after a certain day, and deportation at a proper age. But it was found that the public mind would not bear the proposition, nor will it bear it even at this day. Yet the day is not distant when it must bear and adopt it, or worse will follow. Nothing is more certainly written in the book of fate, than that these people are to be free; nor is it less certain that the two races, equally free, cannot live in the same government. Nature, habit, opinion, have drawn indelible lines of distinction between them. It is still in our power to direct the process of emancipation and deportation peaceably, and in such slow degree as that the evil will wear off insensibly, and their place be, *pari passu*, filled up by free white laborers. If, on the contrary, it is left to force itself on, human nature must shudder at the prospect held up. We should in vain look for an example in the Spanish deportation or deletion of the Moors. This precedent would fall far short of our case." — *Jefferson's Writings*, vol. i. pp. 48, 49.

The opinions on slavery of that pure patriot and able John Jay. statesman, John Jay, the first Chief-Justice of the United- States Supreme Court, appointed by Washington (who so highly appreciated his character and talents, that he tendered him a choice of the offices in his gift), are so well known,

John Jay. that it is not important to cite here any extended extracts from his writings on the subject. Two or three passages from his printed works and his manuscripts will be quite sufficient for my present purpose.

In 1777, Mr. Jay strenuously urged the insertion of an article in the Constitution of the State of New York, adopted in that year, providing for the early abolition of slavery; "so that, in future ages, every human being who breathes the air of this State shall enjoy the privileges of a freeman." — *Flanders's Lives and Times of the Chief Justices*, p. 216.

In 1780, writing from Spain to Egbert Benson, the Attorney-general of New York, Mr. Jay said: —

"An excellent law might be made out of the Pennsylvania one for the gradual abolition of slavery. Till America comes into this measure, her prayers to Heaven for liberty will be impious. This is a strong expression, but it is just. Were I in your Legislature, I would prepare a bill for the purpose with great care; and I would never cease moving it till it became a law, or I ceased to be a member. I believe God governs the world; and I believe it to be a maxim in his as in our court, that those who ask for equity ought to do it." — *Life and Writings of John Jay*, vol. i. 229, 230.

In 1785, Mr. Jay wrote: —

"It is much to be wished that slavery may be abolished. The honor of the States, as well as justice and humanity, in my opinion, loudly call upon them to emancipate these unhappy people. To contend for our own liberty, and to deny that blessing to others, involves an inconsistency not to be excused." — *Idem*, vol. i. p. 231.

In 1786, Mr. Jay drafted a memorial to the Legislature of the State of New York, which commenced with the declaration: —

"Your memorialists, being deeply affected by the situation of those who, although free by the laws of God, are held in slavery by the laws of this State, view with pain and regret the additional miseries which these unhappy people experience from the practice of exporting them, like cattle, to the West Indies and the Southern States."

This memorial was signed by John Jay; Alexander Hamil- John Jay.
ton ; Robert R. Livingston, Chancellor of the State; James
Duane, Mayor of the City of New York; and one hundred
and twenty-nine others, including many eminent civilians and
clergymen. The Constitution of the Manumission Society,
from which this memorial proceeded, declared it to be the
duty of Christians to endeavor to enable the slaves " to share
equally with us in our civil and religious liberty, to which
they are by nature as much entitled as ourselves."

As President of the New-York Manumission Society (an
office held by Mr. Jay until his appointment as Chief-Justice,
when he resigned it, and Alexander Hamilton, Secretary of
the Treasury, was elected in his place), he drafted a public
acknowledgment of an anonymous gift to the treasury of the
Society, of which the following is an extract: —

" What act of public or private justice and philanthropy can
occasion more pleasing emotions in the breasts of Christians, or be
more agreeable to HIM who shed his blood for the redemption of men,
than such as tend to restore the oppressed to their natural rights, and
to raise unfortunate members of the same great family with ourselves
from the abject situation of beasts of burthen, bought and sold and
worked for the benefit and at the pleasure of persons who were not
created more free, more rational, more immortal, nor with more
extensive rights and privileges, than they were." — *From the original
MS. in the Jay Collection at Bedford, N. Y.*

The candid reader cannot fail to contrast these sentiments
of the first Chief-Justice with the assertion of his latest successor, Chief-Justice Taney, that, at the time the Constitution
of the United States was formed, the opinion was "*fixed and
universal in the civilized portion of the white race,*" that the
negro "*had no rights which the white man was bound to
respect.*"

The eminent South-Carolina patriots, Christopher Gadsden
and Henry Laurens, have left their testimony on this subject
in no ambiguous terms.

Christo-
pher
Gadsden.

Mr. Gadsden was one of the most prominent public servants of the South, both in the Continental and the Colonial Legislatures. In a letter to Fr. S. Johnson, in Connecticut, dated at Charleston, S.C., 16th April, 1766, he says,—

" We are a very weak province, a rich growing one, and of as much importance to Great Britain as any upon the continent ; and great part of our weakness (though at the same time 'tis part of our riches) consists in having such a number of slaves amongst us ; and we find in our case, according to the general perceptible workings of Providence, where the crime most commonly though slowly, yet surely, draws a similar and suitable punishment, that slavery begets slavery. Jamaica and our West-India Islands demonstrate this observation, which I hope will not be our case now, whatever might have been the consequences had the fatal attempts been delayed a few years longer, when we had drank deeper of the Circean draught, and the measure of our iniquities were filled up."— *MS*. *Letter* (*printed in the Hist. Mag., Sept.* 1861, p. 261) *in possession of the Hon. George Bancroft.*

Henry
Laurens.

Mr. Laurens was for two years President of the Continental Congress, and afterwards appointed minister to Holland. He was a commissioner, with Franklin and Jay, for negotiating a peace with Great Britain.

Mr. Laurens wrote to his son, from Charleston, S.C., 14th August, 1776 : —

" You know, my dear son, I abhor slavery. I was born in a country where slavery had been established by British kings and parliaments, as well as by the laws of that country, ages before my existence. I found the Christian religion and slavery growing under the same authority and cultivation. I nevertheless disliked it. In former days, there was no combating the prejudices of men supported by interest : the day, I hope, is approaching, when, from principles of gratitude as well as justice, every man will strive to be foremost in showing his readiness to comply with the golden rule. Not less than twenty thousand pounds sterling would all my negroes produce, if sold at public auction to-morrow. I am not the man who enslaved them ; they are indebted to Englishmen for that favor : nevertheless, I am devising means for manumitting many of them, and for cutting off the cutail of slavery. Great powers oppose me, — the laws and Henry
Laurens. customs of my country, my own and the avarice of my countrymen. What will my childreu say if I deprive them of so much estate? These are difficulties, but not insuperable. I will do as much as I can in my time, and leave the rest to a better hand.

"I am not one of those who arrogate the peculiar care of Providence in each fortunate event; nor one of those who dare trust in Providence for defence and security of their own liberty, while they enslave, and wish to continue in slavery, thousands who are as well entitled to freedom as themselves. I perceive the work before me is great. I shall appear to many as a promoter, not only of strange, but of dangerous doctrines: it will therefore be necessary to proceed with caution. You are apparently deeply interested in this affair; but, as I have no doubts concerning your concurrence and approbation, I most sincerely wish for your advice and assistance, and hope to receive both in good time." — *Collection of the Zenger Club,* pp. 20, 21.

Such were the prevailing principles of the people, as Federal
Conven-
tion. expressed by their leading representatives, when the Convention for framing the Federal Constitution assembled in Philadelphia, in May, 1787. It is highly proper that a constant regard should be had to these principles in interpreting the language of the Constitution.

The position and purpose of the Convention were unprecedented. It was the first time in the history of the world that an assemblage of men had been called together, with delegated power from the people, to prepare an instrument which was to establish a Government, and to be the source and test of all their laws.

Some of the delegates to this Convention had been members of the Continental Congress of 1776; and, as was said by John Quincy Adams at the Jubilee of the Constitution in New York, "this act was the complement to the Declaration of Independence; founded upon the same principles, carrying them out into practical execution, and forming with it one entire system of national government."

The Articles of Confederation proved an unsuccessful experiment. When the exigencies of the war were over, and the Government fully assumed the functions of an independent nation, it was seen that an error had been committed in "the substitution of State sovereignty, instead of the constituent sovereignty of the people, as the foundation of the Revolution and of the Union." It is a significant fact, that, in the Preamble to the Constitution, this departure from the principles of the Declaration of Independence is tacitly recognized, and is rectified by a recurrence to the truth, that to secure the rights of life, liberty, and the pursuit of happiness, governments are instituted among men, deriving their just powers from the consent of the governed.

This preamble, of only a single sentence, is the key to the Constitution. Without considering and comprehending it, no one should attempt to interpret any of the separate articles of that instrument.

" WE, THE PEOPLE OF THE UNITED STATES, IN ORDER TO FORM A MORE PERFECT UNION, ESTABLISH JUSTICE, INSURE DOMESTIC TRANQUILLITY, PROVIDE FOR THE COMMON DEFENCE, PROMOTE THE GENERAL WELFARE, AND SECURE THE BLESSINGS OF LIBERTY TO OURSELVES AND OUR POSTERITY, DO ORDAIN AND ESTABLISH THIS CONSTITUTION FOR THE UNITED STATES OF AMERICA."

The Constitution is, and was intended to be, the PEOPLE'S document,— the palladium of their liberty. It was to defend and to bless the negro as well as the white man: for negroes had fought side by side with our white soldiers in the common struggle for liberty ; and, in several of the States, they, as citizens, had voted for the delegates to the Convention, and afterwards on the adoption of the Constitution.

It was established for the purpose of securing *liberty ;* and nothing can be clearer to a careful student of the history of that period, than that the authors of the Declaration of Independence and of the Constitution of the United States, " parts of one consistent whole, founded on one and the same theory of government," believed, that, under their influence and The Constitution and Slavery. operation, slavery would, and they intended that it should, soon be abolished.

It had been declared by Lord Mansfield, in the Court of King's Bench, in England, that slavery was "so odious, that nothing can be suffered to support it but positive law." At the time the Federal Constitution was adopted, there was not, in the State Constitutions, any thing to warrant or justify slavery. Every thing of that kind has come by later amendments. As in the preparation of the Declaration of Independence, so in the formation of the Constitution, the authors did not ignore the existence of slavery. It was an evil that had been forced upon them by Great Britain, against their consent; and was one of the moving causes for the separation from the mother-country. They had, in the most emphatic manner, by resolutions and otherwise, expressed their abhorrence of slavery, and their determination to emancipate the negroes without unnecessary delay. All that the slaveholders asked of the Convention was a *temporary* protection for what they regarded, in one sense, their property, until they could, in their own time and in their own way, bring about this desirable result.

Mr. Pinckney declared, "If the Southern States were let alone, they will probably of themselves stop importations. He would himself, as a citizen of South Carolina, vote for it."

Mr. Sherman observed that "the abolition of slavery seemed to be going on in the United States, and that the good sense of the several States would probably by degrees complete it." Mr. Ellsworth added, — and no one expressed dissent from this opinion, — "Slavery, in time, will not be a speck in our country."

It was an eminent Virginian, Mr. Madison, who declared that "he thought it *wrong* to admit in the Constitution the idea of property in men." That idea was accordingly everywhere scrupulously avoided.

But still, in three separate clauses, the Constitution recognizes the existence of slavery, although it does not permit the word " slave " anywhere to tarnish its text.

"ART. I. SECT. 2. . . . . . Representatives and direct taxes shall be apportioned among the several States which may be included within this Union, according to their respective numbers; which shall be determined by adding to the whole number of free persons, including those bound to service for a term of years, and excluding Indians not taxed, three-fifths of all other persons. . . . .

"ART. I. SECT. 9. The migration or importation of such persons as any of the States now existing shall think proper to admit, shall not be prohibited by the Congress prior to the year one thousand eight hundred and eight ; but a tax or duty may be imposed on such importation, not exceeding ten dollars for each person. . . . .

"ART. IV. SECT. 2. . . . . . No person held to service or labor in one State, under the laws thereof, escaping into another, shall, in consequence of any law or regulation therein, be discharged from such service or labor, but shall be delivered up on claim of the party to whom such service or labor may be due."

In considering these articles in the Convention, the whole subject of slavery was thoroughly discussed. No language of radical reformers in recent times surpasses in severity the honest utterances of the patriots and statesmen who were then assembled. No friendly voice was raised to defend this barbarous crime against humanity. Let us look at some of the speeches.

Mr. Gouverneur Morris, of Pennsylvania, was the member to whom was finally committed the Constitution, to give finish to the style and arrangement of that instrument. He may properly be regarded as the author of its text. In the debate on the 8th of August, 1787, he uses the following language : —

" He never would concur in upholding domestic slavery. It was a nefarious institution. It was the curse of Heaven on the States where it prevailed. Compare the free regions of the Middle States, where a rich and noble cultivation marks the prosperity and happiness of the people, with the misery and poverty which overspread

the barren wastes of Virginia, Maryland, and the other States having
slaves. Travel through the whole continent, and you behold the
prospect continually varying with the appearance and disappearance
of slavery. The moment you leave the Eastern States, and enter
New York, the effects of the institution become visible. Passing
through the Jerseys, and entering Pennsylvania, every criterion of
superior improvement witnesses the change. Proceed southwardly,
and every step you take through the great regions of slaves presents
a desert, increasing with the increasing proportion of these wretched
beings. Upon what principle is it that the slaves shall be computed
in the representation? Are they men? Then make them citizens,
and let them vote. Are they property? Why, then, is no other
property included? The houses in this city (Philadelphia) are worth
more than all the wretched slaves who cover the rice-swamps of
South Carolina. The admission of slaves into the representation,
when fairly explained, comes to this, — that the inhabitant of Georgia
and South Carolina, who goes to the coast of Africa, and, in defiance
of the most sacred laws of humanity, tears away his fellow-creatures
from their dearest connections, and damns them to the most cruel
bondage, shall have more votes in a government instituted for the protection of the rights of mankind than the citizen of Pennsylvania or
New Jersey, who views with a laudable horror so nefarious a practice.
He would add, that domestic slavery is the most prominent feature in
the aristocratic countenance of the proposed Constitution. The vassalage of the poor has ever been the favorite offspring of aristocracy.
And what is the proposed compensation to the Northern States for a
sacrifice of every principle of right, of every impulse of humanity?
They are to bind themselves to march their militia for the defence of
the Southern States, for their defence against those very slaves
of whom they complain. They must supply vessels and seamen in
case of foreign attack. The Legislature will have indefinite power
to tax them by excises and duties on imports, both of which will fall
heavier on them than on the Southern inhabitants; for the bohea tea
used by a Northern freeman will pay more tax than the whole consumption of the miserable slave, which consists of nothing more than
his physical subsistence and the rag that covers his nakedness. On
the other side, the Southern States are not to be restrained from importing fresh supplies of wretched Africans, at once to increase the
danger of attack and the difficulty of defence: nay, they are to be
encouraged to it by an assurance of having their votes in the National

Government increased in proportion; and are, at the same time, to have their exports and their slaves exempt from all contributions for the public service. Let it not be said that direct taxation is to be proportioned to representation. It is idle to suppose that the General Government can stretch its hand directly into the pockets of the people scattered over so vast a country. They can only do it through the medium of exports, imports, and excises. For what, then, are all the sacrifices to be made? He would sooner submit himself to a tax for paying for all the negroes in the United States than saddle posterity with such a Constitution." — *Madison Papers, Elliot*, vol. v. pp. 392, 393.

Mr. Rufus King, of Massachusetts, in the same debate, said : —

"The admission of slaves was a most grating circumstance to his mind, and he believed would be so to a great part of the people of America. He had not made a strenuous opposition to it heretofore, because he had hoped that this concession would have produced a readiness, which had not been manifested, to strengthen the General Government, and to mark a full confidence in it. The report under consideration had, by the tenor of it, put an end to all those hopes. In two great points, the hands of the Legislature were absolutely tied. The importation of slaves could not be prohibited. Exports could not be taxed. Is this reasonable? What are the great objects of the general system? First, defence against foreign invasion; secondly, against internal sedition. Shall all the States, then, be bound to defend each? and shall each be at liberty to introduce a weakness which will render defence more difficult? Shall one part of the United States be bound to defend another part, and that other part be at liberty, not only to increase its own danger, but to withhold the compensation for the burden? If slaves are to be imported, shall not the exports produced by their labor supply a revenue, the better to enable the General Government to defend their masters? There was so much inequality and unreasonableness in all this, that the people of the Northern States could never be reconciled to it. No candid man could undertake to justify it to them. He had hoped that some accommodation would have taken place on this subject; that, at least, a time would have been limited for the importation of slaves. He never could agree to let them be imported without limitation, and then be represented in the National Legislature. Indeed, he could so little persuade himself of the rectitude of such a practice, that he was not sure he could assent to it under any circumstances. At all events, either slaves should not be represented, or exports should be taxable." Debate in the Federal Convention.

Mr. Roger Sherman, of Connecticut, —

" Regarded the slave-trade as iniquitous : but, the point of representation having been settled after much difficulty and deliberation, he did not think himself bound to make opposition ; especially as the present article, as amended, did not preclude any arrangement whatever on that point, in another place of the report." — *Madison Papers, Elliot*, vol. v. 391, 392. Roger Sherman.

Mr. Luther Martin, of Maryland, in the debate, Tuesday, Aug. 21, —

" Proposed to vary Art. 7, Sect. 4, so as to allow a prohibition or tax on the importion of slaves. In the first place, as five slaves are to be counted as three free men in the apportionment of representatives, such a clause would leave an encouragement to this traffic. In the second place, slaves weakened one part of the Union, which the other parts were bound to protect : the privilege of importing them was therefore unreasonable. And, in the third place, it was inconsistent with the principles of the Revolution, and dishonorable to the American character, to have such a feature in the Constitution. Luther Martin.

" Mr. RUTLEDGE did not see how the importation of slaves could be encouraged by this section. He was not apprehensive of insurrections, and would readily exempt the other States from the obligation to protect the Southern against them. Religion and humanity had nothing to do with this question : interest alone is the governing principle with nations. The true question at present is, whether the Southern States shall or shall not be parties to the Union. If the Northern States consult their interest, they will not oppose the increase of slaves, which will increase the commodities of which they will become the carriers. John Rutledge.

" Mr. ELLSWORTH was for leaving the clause as it stands. Let every State import what it pleases. The morality or wisdom of slavery are considerations belonging to the States themselves. What enriches a part enriches the whole, and the States are the best judges of their particular interest. The old Confederation had not meddled with this point ; and he did not see any greater necessity for bringing it within the policy of the new one. Oliver Ellsworth.

" Mr. Pinckney. South Carolina can never receive the plan if it prohibits the slave-trade. In every proposed extension of the powers of Congress, that State has expressly and watchfully excepted that of meddling with the importation of negroes. *If the States be all left at*

liberty on this subject, South Carolina may perhaps, by degrees, do of herself what is wished, as Virginia and Maryland have already done.

" Adjourned.

" WEDNESDAY, Aug. 22.

" *In Convention.* — Art. 7, Sect. 4, was resumed.

" Mr. SHERMAN was for leaving the clause as it stands. He disapproved of the slave-trade; yet, as the States were now possessed of the right to import slaves, as the public good did not require it to be taken from them, and as it was expedient to have as few objections as possible to the proposed scheme of government, he thought it best to leave the matter as we find it. He observed, that *the abolition of slavery seemed to be going on in the United States, and that the good sense of the several States would probably by degrees complete it.* He urged on the Convention the necessity of despatching its business.

" Col. MASON. This infernal traffic originated in the avarice of British merchants. The British Government constantly checked the attempts of Virginia to put a stop to it. The present question concerns, not the importing States alone, but the whole Union. The evil of having slaves was experienced during the late war. Had slaves been treated as they might have been by the enemy, they would have proved dangerous instruments in their hands. But their folly dealt by the slaves as it did by the Tories. He mentioned the dangerous insurrections of the slaves in Greece and Sicily, and the instructions given by Cromwell to the commissioners sent to Virginia, — to arm the servants and slaves, in case other means of obtaining its submission should fail. Maryland and Virginia, he said, had already prohibited the importation of slaves expressly. North Carolina had done the same in substance. All this would be in vain, if South Carolina and Georgia be at liberty to import. The Western people are already calling out for slaves for their new lands; and will fill that country with slaves, if they can be got through South Carolina and Georgia. Slavery discourages arts and manufactures. The poor despise labor when performed by slaves. They prevent the emigration of whites, who really enrich and strengthen a country. *They produce the most pernicious effect on manners. Every master of slaves is born a petty tyrant. They bring the judgment of Heaven on a* country. *As nations cannot be rewarded or punished in the next world, they must be in this. By an inevitable chain of causes and effects, Providence punishes national sins by national calamities.* He lamented that some of our Eastern brethren had, from a lust of gain, embarked in this nefarious traffic. As to the States being in possession of the right to import, this was the case with many other rights, now to be properly given up. He held it essential, in every point of view, that the General Government should have power to prevent the increase of slavery. Debate in the Federal Convention.

" Mr. ELLSWORTH, as he had never owned a slave, could not judge of the effects of slavery on character. He said, however, that, if it was to be considered in a moral light, we ought to go further, and free those already in the country. As slaves also multiply so fast in Virginia and Maryland, that it is cheaper to raise than import them, whilst in the sickly rice-swamps foreign supplies are necessary, if we go no further than is urged, we shall be unjust towards South Carolina and Georgia. Let us not intermeddle. As population increases, poor laborers will be so plenty as to render slaves useless. *Slavery, in time, will not be a speck in our country.* Provision is already made in Connecticut for abolishing it ; and the abolition has already taken place in Massachusetts. As to the danger of insurrections from foreign influence, that will become a motive to kind treatment of the slaves. Oliver Ellsworth.

" Mr. PINCKNEY. If slavery be wrong, it is justified by the example of all the world. He cited the case of Greece, Rome, and other ancient States ; the sanction given by France, England, Holland, and other modern States. In all ages, one-half of mankind have been slaves. *If the Southern States were let alone, they will probably of themselves stop importations. He would himself, as a citizen of South Carolina, vote for it.* An attempt to take away the right, as proposed, will produce serious objections to the Constitution, which he wished to see adopted. Charles Pinckney.

" Gen. PINCKNEY declared it to be his firm opinion, that if himself and all his colleagues were to sign the Constitution, and use their personal influence, it would be of no avail towards obtaining the assent of their constituents. South Carolina and Georgia cannot do without slaves. As to Virginia, she will gain by stopping the importations. Her slaves will rise in value, and she has more than she wants. It would be unequal to require South Carolina and Georgia Charles Cotesworth Pinckney.

8

Debate in the Federal Convention.

to confederate on such unequal terms. He said, the royal assent, before the Revolution, had never been refused to South Carolina as to Virginia. He contended, that the importation of slaves would be for the interest of the whole Union. The more slaves, the more produce to employ the carrying-trade; the more consumption also; and, the more of this, the more revenue for the common treasury. He admitted it to be reasonable, that slaves should be dutied like other imports; but should consider a rejection of the clause as an exclusion of South Carolina from the Union.

Abraham Baldwin.

"Mr. BALDWIN had conceived national objects alone to be before the Convention; not such as, like the present, were of a local nature. Georgia was decided on this point. That State has always hitherto supposed a General Government to be the pursuit of the Central States, who wished to have a vortex for every thing; that her distance would preclude her from equal advantage; and that she could not prudently purchase it by yielding national powers. From this it might be understood in what light she would view an attempt to abridge one of her favorite prerogatives. *If left to herself, she may probably put a stop to the evil.* As one ground for this conjecture, he took notice of the sect of ———, which, he said, was a respectable class of people, who carried their ethics beyond the mere *equality of men*, — extending their humanity to the claims of the whole animal creation.

James Wilson.

"Mr. WILSON observed, that *if South Carolina and Georgia were themselves disposed to get rid of the importation of slaves in a short time, as had been suggested, they would never refuse to unite because the importation might be prohibited.* As the section now stands, all articles imported are to be taxed. Slaves alone are exempt. This is, in fact, a bounty on that article.

Elbridge Gerry.

"Mr. GERRY thought we had nothing to do with the conduct of the States as to slaves, but ought to be careful not to give any sanction to it.

John Dickinson.

"Mr. DICKINSON considered it as inadmissible, on every principle of honor and safety, that the importation of slaves should be authorized to the States by the Constitution. The true question was, whether the national happiness would be promoted or impeded by the importation; and this question ought to be left to the National Government, not to the States particularly interested. If England and France permit slavery, slaves are, at the same time, excluded from both those kingdoms. Greece and Rome were made unhappy by their slaves. He could not believe that the Southern States would Debate in the Federal Conven- tion. refuse to confederate on the account apprehended ; especially as the power was not likely to be immediately exercised by the General Government.

" Mr. WILLIAMSON stated the law of North Carolina on the sub- ject ; to wit, that it did not directly prohibit the importation of slaves. It imposed a duty of £5 on each slave imported from Africa, £10 on each from elsewhere, and £50 on each from a State licensing manu- mission. He thought the Southern States could not be members of the Union, if the clause should be rejected ; and it was wrong to force any thing down not absolutely necessary, and which any State must disagree to.

" Mr. KING thought the subject should be considered in a po- litical light only. If two States will not agree to the Constitution, as stated on one side, he could affirm with equal belief, on the other, that great and equal opposition would be experienced from the other States. He remarked on the exemption of slaves from duty, whilst every other import was subjected to it, as an inequality that could not fail to strike the commercial sagacity of the Northern and Middle States.

" Mr. LANGDON was strenuous for giving the power to the General Government. He could not, with a good conscience, leave it with the States, who could then go on with the traffic, without being restrained by the opinions here given, *that they will themselves cease to import slaves.*

" Gen. PINCKNEY thought himself bound to declare candidly, that he did not think South Carolina would stop her importations of slaves in any short time ; but only stop them occasionally, as she now does. He moved to commit the clause, that slaves might be made liable to an equal tax with other imports ; which he thought right, and which would remove one difficulty that had been started.

" Mr. RUTLEDGE. If the Convention thinks that North Carolina, South Carolina, and Georgia will ever agree to the plan, unless their right to import slaves be untouched, the expectation is vain. The people of those States will never be such fools as to give up so important an interest. He was strenuous against striking out the section, and seconded the motion of Gen. Pinckney for a commit- ment.

" Mr. GOUVERNEUR MORRIS wished the whole subject to be com- mitted, including the clauses relating to taxes on exports and to a

navigation act. These things may form a bargain among the Northern and Southern States.

"Mr. BUTLER declared, that he never would agree to the power of
taxing exports.

"Mr. SHERMAN said it was better to let the Southern States import slaves than to part with them, if they made that a *sine quâ non*.
He was opposed to a tax on slaves imported, as making the matter
worse, because it implied they were *property*. He acknowledged,
that, if the power of prohibiting the importation should be given to
the General Government, it would be exercised. He thought it would
be its duty to exercise the power.

"Mr. READ was for the commitment, provided the clause concerning taxes on exports should also be committed.

"Mr. SHERMAN observed, that that clause had been agreed to, and
therefore could not be committed.

"Mr. RANDOLPH was for committing, in order that some middle
ground might, if possible, be found. He could never agree to the
clause as it stands. He would sooner risk the Constitution. He
dwelt on the dilemma to which the Convention was exposed. By
agreeing to the clause, it would revolt the Quakers, the Methodists,
and many others in the States having no slaves. On the other hand,
two States might be lost to the Union. Let us then, he said, try the
chance of a commitment." —*Madison Papers, Elliot*, vol. v. pp.
457–461.

Three days later (Saturday, Aug. 25th), the debate on this
subject was resumed, and the Report of the Committee of
Eleven was taken up. It was in the following words:—

"Strike out so much of the fourth section as was referred to the
Committee, and insert 'The migration or importation of such persons
as the several States, now existing, think proper to admit, shall not
be prohibited by the Legislature prior to the year 1800 ; but a tax or
duty may be imposed on such migration or importation, at a rate not
exceeding the average of the duties laid on imports.'"

.   .   .   .

"Gen. PINCKNEY moved to strike out the words 'the year eighteen
hundred' as the year limiting the importation of slaves, and to insert
the words 'the year eighteen hundred and eight.'

"Mr. GORHAM seconded the motion.

" Mr. Madison. Twenty years will produce all the mischief that Debate in the Federal Convention. can be apprehended from the liberty to import slaves. So long a term will be more dishonorable to the American character than to say nothing about it in the Constitution.

" On the motion, which passed in the affirmative, —

" New Hampshire, Massachusetts, Connecticut, Maryland, North Carolina, South Carolina, Georgia, ay, — 7; New Jersey, Pennsylvania, Delaware, Virginia, no, — 4.

" Mr. Gouverneur Morris was for making the clause read at once, —

" ' The importation of slaves into North Carolina, South Carolina, and Georgia, shall not be prohibited,' &c.

This, he said, would be most fair, and would avoid the ambiguity by which, under the power with regard to naturalization, the liberty reserved to the States might be defeated. He wished it to be known, also, that this part of the Constitution was a compliance with those States. If the change of language, however, should be objected to by the members from those States, he should not urge it.

" Col. Mason was not against using the term ' slaves,' but against naming North Carolina, South Carolina, and Georgia, lest it should give offence to the people of those States.

" Mr. Sherman liked a description better than the terms proposed, which had been declined by the old Congress, and were not pleasing to some people.

" Mr. Clymer concurred with Mr. Sherman.

" Mr. Williamson said, that, both in opinion and practice, he was against slavery; but thought it more in favor of humanity, from a view of all circumstances, to let in South Carolina and Georgia on those terms, than to exclude them from the Union.

" Mr. Gouverneur Morris withdrew his motion.

" Mr. Dickinson wished the clause to be confined to the States which had not themselves prohibited the importation of slaves; and, for that purpose, moved to amend the clause so as to read, —

" ' The importation of slaves into such of the States as shall permit the same shall not be prohibited by the Legislature of the United States until the year 1808; ' —

which was disagreed to, nem. con.

" The first part of the Report was then agreed to, amended as follows : —

"'The migration or importation of such persons as the several States now existing shall think proper to admit shall not be prohibited by the Legislature prior to the year 1808.'

"New Hampshire, Massachusetts, Connecticut, Maryland, North Carolina, South Carolina, Georgia, ay, — 7; New Jersey, Pennsylvania, Delaware, Virginia, no, — 4." — *Madison Papers, Elliot,* vol. v. pp. 477, 478.

These specimens of the debates are sufficient to show the various shades of opinion as expressed by members of the Convention from different States. The Constitution, with the articles on slavery, as amended and finally adopted by the Federal Convention, was submitted to the people, to be ratified by them through State Conventions of delegates elected for that special purpose. In these State Conventions, the various articles were again thoroughly discussed.

In Massachusetts, the delegates assembled in Boston, Jan. 9th, 1788. It is hardly too much to say, that the fate of the Federal Constitution was to be decided by the action of this State Convention. By the final vote of three hundred and fifty-five members, a majority of only nineteen votes was obtained in its favor; one hundred and eighty-seven being in the affirmative, and one hundred and sixty-eight in the negative. Had the vote been taken without discussion on the first meeting of the members, there can be no doubt that the Constitution would have been rejected by a considerable majority.

Elbridge Gerry, one of our delegates to the Federal Convention, had declined to sign the Constitution, and addressed a letter to the State Legislature, giving his reasons for so doing. He was invited to take a seat with the delegates in the State Convention. John Hancock and Samuel Adams, the two most eminent members of the State Convention, were both opposed to the adoption of the Constitution. Mr. Hancock, on account of his position and from motives of policy, was elected President; but he excused himself from attending until towards the close of the session, on account of illness. The circumstances connected with the change of purpose on

the part of the President are related by Professor Parsons Massachu-setts Con-vention.
in the admirable "Memoir" of his father, Chief-Justice Theophilus Parsons. Amongst the many reasons assigned by the opponents of the Federal Constitution for their desire to defeat its adoption, the articles on the subject of slavery were brought forward. The discussion on this subject deserves our notice.

In the second week of the Convention, (Jan. 17,) the subject of taxation and representation being under debate, "Mr. Wedgery asked, if a boy of six years of age was to be considered as a free person."

The Hon. Rufus King, in answer, said, —

"All persons born free were to be considered as freemen; and, to make the idea of taxation by numbers more intelligible, said that five negro children of South Carolina are to pay as much tax as the three governors of New Hampshire, Massachusetts, and Connecticut." Rufus King.

On the same occasion, Judge Dana spoke: —

"In reply to the remark of some gentlemen, that the Southern States were favored in this mode of apportionment, by having five of their negroes set against three persons in the Eastern, the honorable Judge observed, that the negroes of the Southern States work no longer than when the eye of the driver is on them. 'Can,' asked he, 'that land flourish like this, which is cultivated by the hands of freemen? And are not three of these independent freemen of more real advantage to a State than five of those poor slaves?' As a friend to equal taxation, he rejoiced that an opportunity was presented in this Constitution to change this unjust mode of apportionment. 'Indeed,' concluded he, 'from a survey of every part of the Constitution, I think it the best that the wisdom of man could suggest.'" Francis Dana.

The discussion was continued; and, on the next day, Thomas Dawes, Esq., expressed his views on the subject: —

"Mr. DAWES said, he was sorry to hear so many objections raised against the paragraph under consideration. He thought them wholly unfounded; that the black inhabitants of the Southern States must be considered either as slaves, and as so much property, or in the character of so many free men. If the former, why should they not be wholly Thomas Dawes.

Massachu-
setts Con-
vention.
represented? Our own State laws and Constitution would lead us to consider those blacks as free men; and so, indeed, would our own ideas of natural justice. If, then, they are freemen, they might form an equal basis for representation, as though they were all white inhabitants. In either view, therefore, he could not see that the Northern States would suffer, but directly to the contrary. He thought, however, that gentlemen would do well to connect the passage in dispute with another article in the Constitution, that permits Congress, in the year 1808, wholly to prohibit the importation of slaves, and, in the mean time, to impose a duty of ten dollars a head on such blacks as should be imported before that period. Besides, by the new Constitution, every particular State is left to its own option totally to prohibit the introduction of slaves into its own territories. What could the Convention do more? The members of the Southern States, like ourselves, have *their* prejudices. It would not do to abolish slavery by an act of Congress in a moment, and so destroy what our Southern brethren consider as property; *but we may say, that although slavery is not smitten by an apoplexy, yet it has received a mortal wound, and will die of a consumption.*" — *Debates and Proceedings*, pp. 135–139.

From the minutes of the debates, kept by Chief-Justice Parsons, and printed with the last edition of the " Debates and Proceedings," we learn that George Cabot on this occasion remarked: "The Southern States have the slave-trade, and are sovereign States. *This Constitution is the best way to get rid of it.*"

During the next week (Friday, Jan. 25), the clause relating to "the migration or importation of such persons as any of the States now existing shall think proper to admit" was under consideration; when

James
Neal.
"Mr. NEAL (from Kittery) went over the ground of objection to this section, on the idea that the slave-trade was allowed to be continued for twenty years. His profession, he said, obliged him to bear witness against any thing that should favor the making merchandise of the bodies of men; and, unless his objection was removed, he could not put his hand to the Constitution. Other gentlemen said, in addition to this idea, that there was not even a provision that the negroes ever shall be free; and

"Gen. THOMPSON exclaimed: 'Mr. President, Shall it be said, that, after we have established our own independence and freedom, we make slaves of others? O Washington! What a name has he had! How he has immortalized himself! But he holds those in slavery who have as good right to be free as he has. He is still for self; and, in my opinion, his character has sunk fifty per cent.' Massachu-
setts Con-
vention.

General
Thompson.

"On the other side, gentlemen said, that the step taken in this article towards the abolition of slavery was one of the beauties of the Constitution. They observed that, in the Confederation, there was no provision whatever for its ever being abolished: but this Constitution provides that Congress may, after twenty years, totally annihilate the slave-trade; and that, as all the States, except two, have passed laws to this effect, it might reasonably be expected that it would then be done. In the interim, all the States were at liberty to prohibit it.

"SATURDAY, Jan. 26, 1788.

"The debate on the ninth section still continued desultory, and consisted of similar objections and answers thereto as had before been used. Both sides deprecated the slave-trade in the most pointed terms. On one side, it was pathetically lamented by Mr. Nasson, Major Lusk, Mr. Neal, and others, that this Constitution provided for the continuation of the slave-trade for twenty years; on the other, the Hon. Judge Dana, Mr. Adams, and others, rejoiced that a door was now to be opened for the annihilation of this odious, abhorrent practice, in a certain time." — *Debates and Proceedings*, pp. 208, 209.

On Wednesday, Jan. 30, General Heath, who had been detained by indisposition from attending many of the meetings, was present, and participated in the debate. A part of his remarks were as follows: —

"The paragraph respecting the migration or importation of such persons as any of the States now existing shall think proper to admit, &c., is one of those considered during my absence; and I have heard nothing on the subject, save what has been mentioned this morning. But I think the gentlemen who have spoken have carried the matter rather too far on both sides. General
Heath.

"I apprehend that it is not in our power to do any thing for or against those who are in slavery in the Southern States. No gentleman within these walls detests every idea of slavery more than I do. It is generally detested by the people of this Commonwealth; and I

Massachu-
setts Con-
vention.

ardently hope that the time will soon come, when our brethren in the Southern States will view it as we do, and put a stop to it: but to this we have no right to compel them. Two questions naturally arise : *If we ratify the Constitution, shall we do any thing by our act to hold the blacks in slavery? or shall we become partakers of other men's sins?* I think, neither of them. Each State is sovereign and independent to a certain degree; and they have a right, and will regulate their own internal affairs as to themselves appears proper. And shall we refuse to eat or to drink or to be united with those who do not think or act just as we do? Surely not. We are not, in this case, partakers of other men's sins; for in nothing do we voluntarily encourage the slavery of our fellow-men. A restriction is laid on the Federal Government, which could not be avoided and a union take place. The Federal Convention went as far as they could. The migration, or importation, &c., is confined to the States *now existing* only : new States cannot claim it. Congress, by their ordinance for erecting new States, some time since declared that the new States shall be republican, and that there shall be no slavery in them ; but, whether those in slavery in the Southern States will be emancipated after the year 1808, I do not pretend to determine : I rather doubt it." — *Debates and Proceedings*, pp. 216–217.

One of the longest speeches in the Convention, on the subject of slavery, was made by the Rev. Isaac Backus of Middleborough, on the 4th of February, just before the debates were finally closed. A part of this speech will show its character : —

Isaac
Backus.

"Much, Sir, hath been said about the importation of slaves into this country. I believe, that, according to my capacity, no man abhors that wicked practice more than I do, and would gladly make use of all lawful means toward the abolishing of slavery in all parts of the land. But let us consider where we are, and what we are doing. *In the Articles of Confederation, no provision was made to hinder the importation of slaves into any of these States; but a door is now opened hereafter to do it*, and each State is at liberty now to abolish slavery as soon as they please. And let us remember our former connection with Great Britain, from whom many in our land think we ought not to have revolted. How did they carry on the slave-trade? I know that the Bishop of Gloucester, in an annual

sermon in London in February, 1766, endeavored to justify their Massachusetts Convention.
tyrannical claims of power over us by casting the reproach of the
slave-trade upon the Americans; but, at the close of the war, the
Bishop of Chester, in an annual sermon in February, 1783, ingenu-
ously owned that their nation is the most deeply involved in the guilt
of that trade of any nation in the world, and also that they have
treated their slaves in the West Indies worse than the French or
Spaniards have done theirs. Thus slavery grows more and more
odious through the world; and, as an honorable gentleman said some
days ago, ' *Though we cannot say that slavery is struck with an
apoplexy, yet we may hope it will die with a consumption.*'

. . . . .

"The American Revolution was built upon the principle, that all
men are born with an equal right to liberty and property, and that
officers have no right to any power but what is fairly given them by
the consent of the people. And, in the Constitution now proposed to
us, a power is reserved to the people constitutionally to reduce every
officer again to a private station; and what a guard is this against
their invasion of others' rights, or abusing of their power! Such a
door is now opened for the establishing of righteous government, and
for securing equal liberty, as never was before opened to any people
on earth." — *Debates and Proceedings*, pp. 251, 253.

The final vote on the ratification of the Constitution was Rejoicing on the adoption of the Constitution.
taken on the 6th of February, 1788; and resulted, as has been
already stated, in the affirmative, by the small majority of
nineteen votes. Notwithstanding the strong opposition to it
which was manifested whilst the subject was under discussion,
there was a general acquiescence in the result. The joy of
the people was expressed by enthusiastic public demonstrations. An extract from one of the newspapers of the day will
give a good idea of the popular sentiment at the time: —

"The citizens of Boston have ever shown themselves advocates
for freedom: therefore, when a motion had obtained, one of the
greatest objects of which is ' to secure the blessings of liberty to themselves and their posterity,' they could not resist the strong impulse
they must have had, publicly to testify their gratitude for the pleasing
event. Nor have they. On the decision being declared, the bells in

Celebration in Boston. the several public buildings communicated the happy intelligeuce to every part of the town by a peal, which continued for several hours; and which has been continued, with short intervals, ever since. The discharge of cannon, and other demonstrations of joy, took place on Wednesday and Thursday; but it was left to yesterday to produce an exhibition, to which America has never before witnessed an equal, and which has exceeded any thing of the kind Europe can boast of."— *Columbian Centinel, Feb.* 9, 1788.

New-Hampshire Convention. The published account of the Convention in New Hampshire is very brief and imperfect. The only speech known to have been preserved is here printed entire.

The Hon. Joshua Atherton, from Amherst, spoke as follows : —

Joshua Atherton. "Mr. President, I cannot be of the opinion of the honorable gentlemen who last spoke, that this paragraph is either so useful or so inoffensive as they seem to imagine, or that the objections to it are so totally void of foundation. The idea that strikes those, who are opposed to this clause, so disagreeably and so forcibly, is, hereby it is conceived (if we ratify the Constitution) that we become *consenters to*, and *partakers in*, the sin and guilt of this abominable traffic, at least for a certain period, without any positive stipulation that it should even then be brought to an end. We do not behold in it that valuable acquisition so much boasted of by the honorable member from Portsmouth, ' *that an end is then to be put to slavery.*' Congress may be as much or more puzzled to put a stop to it then than we are now. The clause has not secured its abolition.

"We do not think ourselves under any obligation to perform works of supererogation in the reformation of mankind; we do not esteem ourselves under any necessity to go to Spain or Italy to suppress the Inquisition of those countries, or of making a journey to the Carolinas to abolish the detestable custom of enslaving the Africans : but, Sir, we will not lend the aid of our ratification to this cruel and inhuman merchandise, not even for a day. There is a great distinction in not taking a part in the most barbarous violation of the sacred laws of God and humanity, and our becoming guaranties for its exercise for a term of years. Yes, Sir, it is our full purpose to wash our hands clear of it ; and however unconcerned spectators we may remain of such predatory infractions of the laws of our nature, however unfeelingly we may subscribe to the ratification of man-stealing, with all its baneful consequences, yet I cannot but believe, in justice to human nature, that if we reserve the consideration, and bring this claimed power somewhat nearer to our own doors, we shall form a more equitable opinion of its claim to this ratification. Let us figure to ourselves a company of these man-stealers, well equipped for the enterprise, arriving on our coast. They seize and carry off the whole or a part of the inhabitants of the town of Exeter. Parents are taken, and children left; or possibly they may be so fortunate as to have a whole family taken and carried off together by these relentless robbers. What must be their feelings in the hands of their new and arbitrary masters? Dragged at once from every thing they held dear to them; stripped of every comfort of life, like beasts of prey, — they are hurried on a loathsome and distressing voyage to the coast of Africa, or some other quarter of the globe, where the greatest price may await them; and here, if any thing can be added to their miseries, comes on the heart-breaking scene. A parent is sold to one, a son to another, and a daughter to a third! Brother is cleft from brother, sister from sister, and parents from their darling offspring! Broken with every distress that human nature can feel, and bedewed with tears of anguish, they are dragged into the last stage of depression and slavery, never, never to behold the faces of one another again! The scene is too affecting. I have not fortitude to pursue the subject." — *Elliot's Debates*, vol. ii. pp. 203, 204.

Pennsylvania was the second State to adopt the Constitution. The remarks of James Wilson, in the Ratification Convention, must not be omitted. Mr. Wilson was one of the signers of the Declaration of Independence, and was for several years a member of Congress. He was not only an eloquent orator and ready debater, but may be regarded as one of the first jurists in the country. Washington appointed him a Judge of the Supreme Court of the United States the year after the adoption of the Constitution; and he held the office until his death, which occurred in 1798. The opinions of such a man are entitled to great consideration.

New-Hampshire Convention.

Joshua Atherton.

Pennsylvania Convention.

" With respect to the clause restricting Congress from prohibiting the *migration or importation of such persons* as any of the States now existing shall think proper to admit prior to the year 1808, the honorable gentleman says that this clause is not only dark, but intended to grant to Congress, for that time, the power to admit the importion of *slaves*. No such thing was intended. But I will tell you what was done, and it gives me high pleasure that so much was done. Under the present Confederation, the States may admit the importation of slaves as long as they please; but by this article, after the year 1808, the Congress will have power to prohibit such importation, notwithstanding the disposition of any State to the contrary. *I consider this as laying the foundation for banishing slavery out of this country; and though the period is more distant than I could wish, yet it will produce the same kind, gradual change which was pursued in Pennsylvania.* It is with much satisfaction I view this power in the General Government, whereby they may lay an interdiction on this reproachful trade. But an immediate advantage is also obtained : for a tax or duty may be imposed on such importation, not exceeding ten dollars for each person ; and this, Sir, operates as a partial prohibition. It was all that could be obtained. I am sorry it was no more ; but from this I think there is reason to hope, that yet a few years, and it will be prohibited altogether; and, in the mean time, the *new* States which are to be formed will be under *the control* of Congress in this particular, and slaves will never be introduced amongst them.

.   .   .   .   .

"I recollect, on a former day, the honorable gentleman from Westmoreland (Mr. Findley), and the honorable gentleman from Cumberland (Mr. Whitehill), took exceptions against the 1st clause of the 9th sect., art. 1, arguing, very unfairly, that, because Congress, might impose a tax or duty of ten dollars on the importation of slaves' within any of the United States, Congress might therefore permit slaves to be imported within this State, contrary to its laws. I confess, I little thought that this part of the system would be excepted to.

"I am sorry that it could be extended no farther ; but, so far as it operates, it presents us with the pleasing prospect, that the rights of mankind will be acknowledged and established throughout the Union.

"If there was no other lovely feature in the Constitution but this one, it would diffuse a beauty over its whole countenance. *Yet the lapse of a few years, and Congress will have power to exterminate slavery from within our borders.*" — *Elliot's Debates*, vol. ii. pp. 452, 484. James Wilson.

Maryland adopted the Constitution in opposition to the strong remonstrance of Luther Martin. The address which he made to the State Legislature has been published, and fills between forty and fifty closely printed pages. The part pertinent to this paper is here copied entire : — Maryland Legislature.

"By the ninth section of this article, the importation of such persons as any of the States now existing shall think proper to admit shall not be prohibited prior to the year one thousand eight hundred and eight ; but a duty may be imposed on such importation, not exceeding ten dollars each person. Luther Martin to the Legislature of Maryland.

"The design of this clause is to prevent the General Government from prohibiting the importation of slaves : but the same reasons which caused them to strike out the word 'national,' and not admit the word 'stamps,' influenced them here to guard against the word 'slaves.' They anxiously sought to avoid the admission of expressions which might be odious in the ears of Americans, although they were willing to admit into their system those things which the expressions signified : and hence it is that the clause is so worded as really to authorize the General Government to impose a duty of ten dollars on every foreigner who comes into a State to become a citizen, whether he comes absolutely free, or qualifiedly so as a servant ; although this is contrary to the design of the framers, and the duty was only meant to extend to the importation of slaves.

"This clause was the subject of a great diversity of sentiment in the Convention. As the system was reported by the committee of detail, the provision was general, that such importation should not be prohibited, without confining it to any particular period. This was rejected by eight States; Georgia, South Carolina, and, I think, North Carolina, voting for it.

"We were then told by the delegates of the two first of those States, that their States would never agree to a system which put it in the power of the General Government to prevent the importation of slaves ; and that they, as delegates from those States, must withhold their assent from such a system.

"A committee of one member from each State was chosen by ballot to take this part of the system under their consideration, and to endeavor to agree upon some report which should reconcile those States. To this committee also was referred the following proposition, which had been reported by the committee of detail; viz., 'No navigation act shall be passed without the assent of two-thirds of the members present in each house,'—a proposition which the staple and commercial States were solicitous to retain, lest their commerce should be placed too much under the power of the Eastern States, but which these last States were as anxious to reject. This committee, of which also I had the honor to be a member, met, and took under their consideration the subjects committed to them. I found the Eastern States, notwithstanding their aversion to slavery, were very willing to indulge the Southern States at least with a temporary liberty to prosecute the slave-trade, provided the Southern States would, in their turn, gratify them by laying no restriction on navigation acts; and, after a very little time, the committee, by a great majority, agreed on a report, by which the General Government was to be prohibited from preventing the importation of slaves for a limited time, and the restrictive clause relative to navigation acts was to be omitted.

"This report was adopted by a majority of the Convention, but not without considerable opposition. It was said that we had just assumed a place among independent nations in consequence of our opposition to the attempts of Great Britain to enslave us; that this opposition was grounded upon the preservation of those rights to which God and nature had entitled us, not in particular, but in common with the rest of all mankind; that we had appealed to the Supreme Being for his assistance, as the God of freedom, who could not but approve our efforts to preserve the rights which he had thus imparted to his creatures; that now, when we scarcely had risen from our knees, from supplicating his aid and protection in forming our government over a free people,—a government formed pretendedly on the principles of liberty, and for its preservation,—in that government to have a provision not only putting it out of its power to restrain and prevent the slave-trade, but even encouraging that most infamous traffic by giving the States power and influence in the Union in proportion as they cruelly and wantonly sport with the rights of their fellow-creatures, ought to be considered as a solemn mockery of, and insult to, that God whose protection we had then implored; and could not fail to hold us up in detestation, and render us contemptible to every true friend of liberty in the world. It was said, it ought to be considered that national crimes can only be, and frequently are, punished in this world by national punishments; and that the continuance of the slave-trade, and thus giving it a national sanction and encouragement, ought to be considered as justly exposing us to the displeasure and vengeance of Him who is equally Lord of all, and who views with equal eye the poor African slave and his American master. *Luther Martin to the Legislature of Maryland.*

" It was urged, that, by this system, we were giving the General Government full and absolute power to regulate commerce; under which general power it would have a right to restrain, or totally prohibit, the slave-trade. It must therefore appear to the world absurd and disgraceful, to the last degree, that we should except from the exercise of that power the only branch of commerce which is unjustifiable in its nature, and contrary to the rights of mankind; that, on the contrary, we ought rather to prohibit expressly, in our Constitution, the further importation of slaves, and to authorize the General Government, from time to time, to make such regulations as should be thought most advantageous for the gradual abolition of slavery, and the emancipation of the slaves which are already in the States; that slavery is inconsistent with the genius of republicanism, and has a tendency to destroy those principles on which it is supported, as it lessens the sense of the equal rights of mankind, and habituates us to tyranny and oppression. It was further urged, that, by this system of government, every State is to be protected both from foreign invasion and from domestic insurrections; that, from this consideration, it was of the utmost importance it should have a power to restrain the importation of slaves, since, in proportion as the number of slaves was increased in any State, in the same proportion the State is weakened, and exposed to foreign invasion or domestic insurrection, and by so much less will it be able to protect itself against either; and therefore will, by so much the more, want aid from, and be a burden to, the Union. It was further said, that as, in this system, we were giving the General Government a power, under the idea of national character or national interest, to regulate even our weights and measures, and have prohibited all possibility of emitting paper money, and passing insolvent laws, &c., it must appear still more extraordinary that we should prohibit the government from interfering with the slave-trade, than which nothing could so ma-

Luther
Martin to
the Legis-
lature of
Maryland.

terially affect both our national honor aud interest. These reasons influenced me, both on the Committee and in Convention, most decidedly to oppose and vote against the clause, as it now makes a part of the system.

"You will perceive, Sir, not only that the General Government is prohibited from interfering in the slave-trade before the year eighteen hundred and eight, but that there is no provision in the Constitution that it shall afterwards be prohibited, nor any security that such prohibition will ever take place ; and I think there is great reason to believe, that, if the importation of slaves is permitted until the year eighteen hundred and eight, it will not be prohibited after-wards. At this time, we do not generally hold this commerce in so great abhorrence as we have done. When our liberties were at stake, we warmly felt for the common rights of men. The danger being thought to be past which threatened ourselves, we are daily growing more insensible to those rights. In those States which have restrained or prohibited the importation of slaves, it is only done by legislative acts which may be repealed. When those States find that they must, in their national character and connection, suffer in the disgrace, and share in the inconveniences, attendant upon that detestable and iniquitous traffic, they may be desirous also to share in the benefits arising from it ; and the odium attending it will be greatly effaced by the sanction which is given to it in the General Government." — *Elliot's Debates*, vol. i. pp. 372–375.

Virginia
Conven-
tion.

Virginia was the tenth State to ratify the Constitution. Nowhere were the debates more able and thorough than there. It was not till June that the Convention was held. The proceedings occupy the whole of the third volume of Elliot's "Debates." George Mason, Patrick Henry, and James Madison were among the most important speakers. Let us look at their speeches.

"TUESDAY, June 15, 1788.

George
Mason.

"Mr. GEORGE MASON. Mr. Chairman, this is a fatal section, which has created more dangers than any other. The first clause allows the importation of slaves for twenty years. Under the Royal Government, this evil was looked upon as a great oppression, and many attempts were made to prevent it ; but the interest of the African merchants prevented its prohibition. No sooner did the Revolution take place than it was thought of. It was one of the great causes of our separation from Great Britain. Its exclusion has been a principal object of this State, and most of the States in the Union. The augmentation of slaves weakens the States; *and such a trade is diabolical in itself, and disgraceful to mankind :* yet, by this Constitution, it is continued for twenty years. As much as I value a union of all the States, *I would not admit the Southern States into the Union, unless they agree to the discontinuance of this disgraceful trade, because it would bring weakness, and not strength, to the Union.* And, though this infamous traffic be continued, we have no security for the property of that kind which we have already. There is no clause in this Constitution to secure it; *for they may lay such a tax as will amount to manumission.* And should the Government be amended, still this detestable kind of commerce cannot be discontinued till after the expiration of twenty years; for the fifth article, which provides for amendments, expressly excepts this clause. *I have ever looked upon this as a most disgraceful thing to America.* I cannot express my detestation of it. Yet they have not secured us the property of the slaves we have already : so that ' they have done what they ought not to have done, and have left undone what they ought to have done.'

"Mr. MADISON. Mr. Chairman, I should conceive this clause to be impolitic, if it were one of those things which could be excluded without encountering greater evils. The Southern States would not have entered into the Union of America, without the *temporary* permission of that trade; and, if they were excluded from the Union, the consequences might be dreadful to them and to us. We are not in a worse situation than before. That traffic is prohibited by our laws, and we may continue the prohibition. The Union in general is not in a worse situation. Under the Articles of Confederation, it might be continued for ever; but, by this clause, an end may be put to it after twenty years. There is, therefore, an amelioration of our circumstances. A tax may be laid in the mean time : but it is limited; otherwise Congress might lay such a tax as would amount to a prohibition. From the mode of representation and taxation, Congress cannot lay such a tax on slaves as will amount to manumission. Another clause secures us that property which we now possess. At present, if any slave elopes to any of those States where slaves are free, he becomes emancipated by their laws; for the laws of the States are uncharitable to one another in this respect. But, in this Constitution, ' no person held to service or labor in one State, under the laws

margin notes: Virginia Convention. — George Mason. — James Madison.

thereof, escaping into another, shall, in consequence of any law or regulation therein, be discharged from such service or labor; but shall be delivered up on claim of the party to whom such service or labor shall be due.' This clause was expressly inserted to enable owners of slaves to reclaim them.

"This is a better security than any that now exists. No power is given to the General Government to interpose with respect to the property in slaves now held by the States. The taxation of this State being equal only to its representation, such a tax cannot be laid as he supposes. They cannot prevent the importation of slaves for twenty years; but, after that period, they can. The gentlemen from South Carolina and Georgia argued in this manner: 'We have now liberty to import this species of property; and much of the property now possessed had been purchased, or otherwise acquired, in contemplation of improving it by the assistance of imported slaves. What would be the consequence of hindering us from it? The slaves of Virginia would rise in value, and we should be obliged to go to your markets.' I need not expatiate on this subject. Great as the evil is, a dismemberberment of the Union would be worse. If those States should disunite from the other States for not indulging them in the temporary continuance of this traffic, they might solicit and obtain aid from foreign powers.

"Mr. TYLER warmly enlarged on the impolicy, iniquity, and disgracefulness of this wicked traffic. He thought the reasons urged by gentlemen in defence of it were inconclusive and ill-founded. It was one cause of the complaints against British tyranny, that this trade was permitted. The Revolution had put a period to it; but now it was to be revived. He thought nothing could justify it. This temporary restriction on Congress militated, in his opinion, against the arguments of gentlemen on the other side, that what was not given up was retained by the States; for that, if this restriction had not been inserted, Congress could have prohibited the African trade. The power of prohibiting it was not expressly delegated to them; yet they would have had it by implication, if this restraint had not been provided. This seemed to him to demonstrate most clearly the necessity of restraining them, by a Bill of Rights, from infringing our unalienable rights. It was immaterial whether the Bill of Rights was by itself, or included in the Constitution. But he contended for it one way or the other. It would be justified by our own example and that of England. His earnest desire was, that it should be handed down

to posterity that he had opposed this wicked clause." — *Elliot's De-* Virginia Convention.
bates, vol. iii. pp. 452–454.

Patrick Henry was the most distinguished opponent of the Federal Constitution in the whole country. He had been appointed a delegate to the Convention at Philadelphia, but declined to attend. In the Virginia State Convention he persistently endeavored to defeat its adoption. When he found his efforts unsuccessful, like a true patriot, he ceased his opposition. Although he detested slavery, he was unwilling to grant to the United-States Congress the power of abolishing it without the consent of the States. This power he thought he saw in the Constitution, though not directly expressed in its language.

"Among ten thousand implied powers which they may assume, Patrick Henry. they may, if we be engaged in war, liberate every one of your slaves, if they please; and this must and will be done by men, a majority of whom have not a common interest with you. They will, therefore, have no feeling of your interests. It has been repeatedly said here, that the great object of a National Government was national defence. That power which is said to be intended for security and safety may be rendered detestable and oppressive. If they give power to the General Government to provide for the general defence, the means must be commensurate to the end. All the means in the possession of the people must be given to the Government which is intrusted with the public defence. In this State, there are 236.000 blacks, and there are many in several other States : but there are few or none in the Northern States ; and yet, if the Northern States shall be of opinion that our slaves are numberless, they may call forth every national resource. May Congress not say *that every black man must fight?* Did we not see a little of this last war ? We were not so hard pushed as to make emancipation general ; but acts of Assembly passed, that every slave who would go to the army should be free. Another thing will contribute to bring this event about: slavery is detested ; we feel its fatal effects; we deplore it with all the pity of humanity. Let all these considerations, at some future period, press with full force on the minds of Congress, — let that urbanity, which I trust will distinguish America, and the necessity of national defence, — let

Virginia Convention.

Patrick Henry.

all these things operate on their minds: they will search that paper, and see if they have power of manumission. And have they not, Sir? Have they not power to provide for the general defence and welfare? May they not think that these call for the abolition of slavery? May they not pronounce all slaves free? and will they not be warranted by that power? This is no ambiguous implication or logical deduction. The paper speaks to the point. They have the power, in clear, unequivocal terms, and will clearly and certainly exercise it. As much as I deplore slavery, I see that prudence forbids its abolition. I deny that the General Government ought to set them free, because a decided majority of the States have not the ties of sympathy and fellow-feeling for those whose interest would be affected by their emancipation. The majority of Congress is to the North, and the slaves are to the South." — *Elliot's Debates*, vol. iii. pp. 589, 590.

Governor Randolph had been a member of the Federal Convention; but he had refused to sign the Constitution, wishing to be left free to oppose or to advocate its adoption when it came before his State for consideration. He afterwards, however, saw, that on the ratification of the Constitution hung all hopes of preserving the Union, and he now gave it his hearty support. He thus replied to Mr. Henry: —

Edmund Randolph.

"That honorable gentleman, and some others, have insisted that the abolition of slavery will result from it, and at the same time have complained that it encourages its continuation. The inconsistency proves, in some degree, the futility of their arguments. But, if it be not conclusive to satisfy the committee that there is no danger of enfranchisement taking place, I beg leave to refer them to the paper itself. I hope that there is none here, who, considering the subject in the calm light of philosophy, will advance an objection dishonorable to Virginia, — *that, at the moment they are securing the rights of their citizens, an objection is started that there is a spark of hope that those unfortunate men now held in bondage may, by the operation of the General Government, be made free.* But, if any gentleman be terrified by this apprehension, let him read the system. I ask, and I will ask again and again, till I be answered (not by declamation), *Where* is the part that has a tendency to *the abolition of slavery?* Is it the clause which says that ' the migration or importation of such persons as any of the States now existing shall think proper to admit shall *Virginia* not be prohibited by Congress prior to the year 1808'? This is an *Convention*. exception from the power of regulating commerce, and the restriction is only to continue till 1808. Then Congress can, by the exercise of *Edmund Randolph*. that power, prevent future importations. But does it affect the existing state of slavery? Were it right here to mention what passed in convention on the occasion, I might tell you *that the Southern States, even South Carolina herself, conceived this property to be secure by these words.* I believe, whatever we may think here, that there was not a member of the Virginia delegation who had *the smallest suspicion of the abolition of slavery.* Go to their meaning. Point out the clause where this formidable power of emancipation is inserted." — *Elliot's Debates,* vol. iii. pp. 598, 599.

In North Carolina, a Convention, " for the purpose of de- *North-Carolina* liberating and determining on the proposed Constitution," *Convention.* was called by the Legislature. It assembled in Hillsborough on the 21st of July, 1788; and continued its session till Aug. 2d, when it adjourned without either adopting or rejecting the Constitution.

A few extracts from the debates will show how slavery was regarded in its connection with the Federal Constitution.

" Mr. DAVIE. . . . The gentleman ' does not wish to be represent- *William R.* ed with negroes.' This, Sir, is an unhappy species of population; *Davie.* but we cannot at present alter their situation. The Eastern States had great jealousies on this subject. They insisted that their cows and horses were equally entitled to representation; that the one was property as well as the other. It became our duty, on the other hand, to acquire as much weight as possible in the legislation of the Union; and, as the Northern States were more populous in whites, this only could be done by insisting that a certain proportion of our slaves should make a part of the computed population. It was attempted to form a rule of representation from a compound ratio of wealth and population: but, on consideration, it was found impracticable to determine the comparative value of lands and other property, in so extensive a territory, with any degree of accuracy; and population alone was adopted as the only practicable rule or criterion of representation. It was urged by the deputies of the Eastern States, that a representation of two-fifths would be of little utility, and that

North-
Carolina
Convention.

William R.
Davie.

their entire representation would be unequal and burdensome; that, in a time of war, slaves rendered a country more vulnerable, while its defence devolved upon its free inhabitants. On the other hand, we insisted, that, in time of peace, they contributed, by their labor, to the general wealth, as well as other members of the community; that, *as rational beings, they had a right of representation, and, in some instances, might be highly useful in war.* On these principles, the Eastern States gave the matter up, and consented to the regulation as it has been read. I hope these reasons will appear satisfactory."—*Elliot's Debates,* vol. iv. pp. 30, 31.

When the ninth section was under discussion, Mr. M'Dowall wished to hear the reasons of the restriction on Congress in regard to prohibiting the importation of slaves before the year 1808.

Richard D.
Spaight.

"Mr. SPAIGHT answered, that there was a contest between the Northern and Southern States; that the Southern States, whose principal support depended on the labor of slaves, would not consent to the desire of the Northern States to exclude the importation of slaves absolutely; that South Carolina and Georgia insisted on this clause, as they were now in want of hands to cultivate their lands; that, in the course of twenty years, they would be fully supplied; that the trade would be abolished then; and that, in the mean time, some tax or duty might be laid on.

Joseph
M'Dowall.

"Mr. M'DOWALL replied, that the explanation was just such as he expected, and by no means satisfactory to him; and that he looked upon it as a very objectionable part of the system.

James
Iredell.

"Mr. IREDELL. Mr. Chairman, I rise to express sentiments similar to those of the gentleman from Craven. For my part, were it practicable to put an end to the importation of slaves immediately, it would give me the greatest pleasure; for it certainly is a trade utterly inconsistent with the rights of humanity, and under which great cruelties have been exercised. *When the entire abolition of slavery takes place, it will be an event which must be pleasing to every generous mind and every friend of human nature; but we often wish for things which are not attainable. It was the wish of a great majority of the Convention to put an end to the trade immediately; but the States of South Carolina and Georgia would not agree to it.* Consider, then, what would be the difference between our present situation in this

respect, if we do not agree to the Constitution, and what it will be if North-Carolina
we do agree to it.　If we do not agree to it, do we remedy the evil? Conven-
No, Sir: we do not; for, if the Constitution be not adopted, it will tion.
be in the power of every State to continue it for ever.　They may or
may not abolish it at their discretion.　But, if we adopt the Constitu- James Iredell.
tion, the trade must cease after twenty years, if Congress declare so,
whether particular States please so or not: surely, then, we can gain
by it.　This was the utmost that could be obtained.　I heartily wish
more could have been done; but, as it is, this Government is nobly
distinguished above others by that very provision.　Where is there
another country in which such a restriction prevails?　We therefore,
Sir, set an example of humanity, by providing for the abolition of
this inhuman traffic, though at a distant period.　I hope, therefore,
that this part of the Constitution will not be condemned because it
has not stipulated for what was impracticable to obtain.

　　　　·　　　　·　　　　·　　　　·

"Mr. GALLOWAY.　Mr. Chairman, the explanation given to this James Galloway
clause does not satisfy my mind.　I wish to see this abominable trade
put an end to.　But in case it be thought proper to continue this
abominable traffic for twenty years, yet I do not wish to see the tax
on the importation extended to all persons whatsoever.　Our situation
is different from the people to the North.　We want citizens: they
do not.　Instead of laying a tax, we ought to give a bounty to encourage foreigners to come among us.　With respect to the abolition
of slavery, it requires the utmost consideration.　The property of the
Southern States consists principally of slaves.　If they mean to do
away slavery altogether, this property will be destroyed.　I apprehend it means to bring forward manumission.　If we must manumit
our slaves, what country shall we send them to?　It is impossible
for us to be happy, if, after manumission, they are to stay among us.

"Mr. IREDELL. . . . . There is another circumstance to be ob- James Iredell.
served.　There is no authority vested in Congress to restrain the
States, in the interval of twenty years, from doing what they please.
If they wish to prohibit such importation, they may do so." — Elliot's
Debates, vol. iv. pp. 100–102.

　　In South Carolina, the Constitution was discussed in the South-Carolina
Legislature before the Convention was called.　Two or three Legisla-ture.
extracts from the speeches made before that body will end
these specimens of the Debates.

South-
Carolina
Legisla-
ture.

Rawlins
Lowndes.

"Mr. Lowndes remarked, that we had a law prohibiting the importation of negroes for three years, — a law he greatly approved of; but there was no reason offered why the Southern States might not find it necessary to alter their conduct, and open their ports. *Without negroes, this State would degenerate into one of the most contemptible in the Union;* and he cited an expression that fell from General Pinckney on a former debate, that, whilst there remained one acre of swamp-land in South Carolina, he should raise his voice against restricting the importation of negroes. Even in granting the importation for twenty years, care had been taken to make us pay for this indulgence; each negro being liable, on importation, to pay a duty not exceeding ten dollars; and, in addition to this, they were liable to a capitation tax. Negroes were our wealth, our only natural resource; yet behold how our kind friends in the North were determined soon to tie up our hands, and drain us of what we had! The Eastern States drew their means of subsistence, in a great measure, from their shipping; and, on that head, they had been particularly careful not to allow of any burdens. They were not to pay tonnage or duties; no, not even the form of clearing out: all ports were free and open to them! Why, then, call this a reciprocal bargain, which took all from one party, to bestow it on the other?" — *Elliot's Debates*, vol. iv. pp. 272, 273.

General Charles Cotesworth Pinckney had been a member of the Federal Convention, and was an earnest and able supporter of the rights of the State he represented. He was undoubtedly sincere in his belief that he had made for his constituents pretty good terms in regard to their special interests, and that they ought to be satisfied with the Constitution, and vote for its adoption.

Gen. C. C.
Pinckney.

"You have so frequently heard my sentiments on this subject, that I need not now repeat them. It was alleged by some of the members who opposed an unlimited importation, that slaves increased the weakness of any State who admitted them; that they were a dangerous species of property, which an invading enemy could easily turn against ourselves and the neighboring States; and that, as we were allowed a representation for them in the House of Representatives, our influence in government would be increased in proportion as we were less able to defend ourselves. 'Show some period,' said the members from the Eastern States, 'when it may be in our power to put a stop, if we please, to the importation of this weakness, and we will endeavor, for your convenience, to restrain the religious and political prejudices of our people on this subject.' The Middle States and Virginia made us no such proposition: they were for an immediate and total prohibition. We endeavored to obviate the objections that were made, in the best manner we could, and assigned reasons for our insisting on the importation; which there is no occasion to repeat, as they must occur to every gentleman in the house. A Committee of the States was appointed, in order to accommodate this matter; and, after a great deal of difficulty, it was settled on the footing recited in the Constitution. *{South-Carolina Legislature. Gen. C. C. Pinckney.}*

" By this settlement, we have secured an unlimited importation of negroes for twenty years. Nor is it declared that the importation shall be then stopped: it may be continued. We have a security that the General Government can never emancipate them; for no such authority is granted: and it is admitted, on all hands, that the General Government has no powers but what are expressly granted by the Constitution, and that all rights not expressed were reserved by the several States. We have obtained a right to recover our slaves in whatever part of America they may take refuge; which is a right we had not before. In short, considering all circumstances, we have made the best terms for the security of this species of property it was in our power to make. We would have made better, if we could; but, on the whole, I do not think them bad." — *Elliot's Debates*, vol. iv. pp. 285, 286.

Outside, also, of the State Conventions, opinions in regard to the effect of the Federal Constitution on slavery were divided. Two letters, written on the same day, in different parts of the country, by persons of high character and great influence in their respective States, will exhibit these differing views.

Dr. Ramsay, the historian of South Carolina, in a letter to General Lincoln, dated Charleston, Jan. 29th, 1788, says, —

" Our Assembly is now sitting, and have unanimously agreed to hold a convention. By common consent, the merits of the Federal Constitution were freely discussed on that occasion, for the sake of *{Doctor Ramsay.}*

enlightening our citizens. Mr. [Rawlins] Lowndes was the only man who made direct, formal opposition to it. His objections were local, and proceeded from an illiberal jealousy of New-England men. He urged that you would raise freights on us, and, in short, that you were too cunning for our honest people; that your end of the Continent would rule the other; and that the sun of our glory would set when the new Constitution operated. He has not one Federal idea in his head. He is said to be honest, and free from debt: but he was an enemy to independence; and, though our President in 1778, he was a British subject in 1780. His taking protection was rather the passive act of an old man than otherwise. He never aided or abetted the British Government directly; but his example was mischievous. His opposition has poisoned the minds of some.

"I fear the numerous class of debtors more than any other. On the whole, I have no doubt the Constitution will be accepted by a very great majority in this State. The sentiments of our leading men are, of late, much more Federal than formerly. This honest sentiment was avowed by the first characters: 'New England has lost, and we have gained, by the war; and her suffering citizens ought to be our carriers, though a dearer freight should be the consequence.' Your delegates never did a more politic thing than in standing by those of South Carolina about negroes. Virginia deserted them, and was for an immediate stoppage of further importation. The [Old] Dominion has lost much popularity by the conduct of her delegates on this head. The language now is, 'The Eastern States can soonest help us in case of invasion; and it is more our interest to encourage them and their shipping than to join with or look up to Virginia.'

"In short, Sir, a revolution highly favorable to union has taken place: Federalism, and liberality of sentiment, have gained great ground. Mr. Lowndes still thinks you are a set of sharpers, and does not wonder that you are for the new Constitution; as, in his opinion, you will have all the advantage. He thinks you begrudge us our negroes. But he is almost alone." — *Bowen's Life of Gen. Lincoln,* (*Sparks's Amer. Biogr.,* 2d Series, vol. xiii.,) pp. 410–412.

In a letter to Dr. Hart of Preston, dated 29th January, 1788, the Rev. Dr. Hopkins of Newport, R.I., writes thus:—

"The new Constitution, you observe, guarantees this trade for twenty years. I fear, if it be adopted, this will prove an Achan in

our camp. How does it appear in the sight of Heaven and of all Rev. Dr. Hopkins.
good men, well informed, that *these States*, who have been fighting
for liberty, and consider themselves as the highest and most noble
example of zeal for it, cannot agree in any political Constitution,
unless it indulge and authorize them to enslave their fellow-men!
I think if this Constitution be not adopted as it is, without any alteration, we shall have none, and shall be in a state of anarchy, and
probably of civil war. Therefore I wish to have it adopted; but
still, as I said, *I fear.* And perhaps civil war will not be avoided, if
it be adopted. Ah! these unclean spirits, like frogs, — they, like the
Furies of the poets, are spreading discord, and exciting men to con-
tention and war, wherever they go; and they can spoil the best
Constitution that can be formed. When Congress shall be formed on
the new plan, these frogs will be there; for they go forth to the kings
of the earth, in the first place. They will turn the members of that
august body into devils, so far as they are permitted to influence them.
Have they not already got possession of most of the men who will or
can be chosen and appointed to a place in that assembly? I suppose
that even good Christians are not out of the reach of influence from
these frogs. 'Blessed is he that watcheth and keepeth his garments.'" — *Park's Memoir of Hopkins*, pp. 158, 159.

I have thus attempted to give a fair representation of the
different shades of opinion on the Constitution in its relations
to slavery, as expressed by the leading statesmen at the North
and at the South. In the ample extracts from the Debates
which have been presented, an apparent lack of harmony may
be discovered among the arguments used in various parts of
the country, whether in urging its adoption or its rejection.
With an earnest zeal to secure for their country so great a
boon as a firmly established Constitutional Government, its
advocates may have pressed a little too strongly the arguments in favor of the views most acceptable to the particular
State which at the time had the matter under consideration.
On the other hand, the opponents of the Constitution undoubtedly exaggerated the evils which it was supposed it would
entail upon the States, and perhaps unconsciously misrepre-
sented the effects of the different clauses referring to slavery.

One thing is certain, that whilst the delegates from Georgia and South Carolina asked only a temporary toleration of the slave-trade, and non-interference with their local arrangements respecting domestic slavery, (declaring that, if let alone, they might themselves, as soon as it was practicable, stop the importation of slaves,) the common sentiment, in the Convention and throughout the country, was, that the letter and the spirit of the Constitution, fairly interpreted and faithfully applied, afforded a full guaranty of universal freedom throughout the Union at no distant day. The purpose of the Constitution was put into the preamble in no equivocal language, and for no doubtful purpose. It was "TO SECURE LIBERTY," and not to protect slavery: for liberty had been declared to be a natural, national, and unalienable right; while slavery was known to be an unnatural, sectional, temporary evil. It was intended, that, under the Constitution, slavery should, and it was expected that it would, at no distant day, be abolished.

The distinguished English moralist, Dr. Paley, published his "Moral and Political Philosophy" two years after our National Independence had been acknowledged. In his chapter on Slavery, he placed permanently on record his view of the effect of the principles promulgated by the American patriots, in these words: "The great Revolution which has taken place in the Western World may probably conduce (and who knows but that it was designed?) to accelerate the fall of this abominable tyranny."

Half a century later, in the Senate of the United States, Daniel Webster, the great defender of the Constitution, reaffirmed the principles of the Founders of the Republic in an immortal sentence, which it would be well for his countrymen now to heed. It is applicable in a broader sense than its author on that occasion intended: "LIBERTY AND UNION, NOW AND FOR EVER, ONE AND INSEPARABLE."

II.

NEGROES AS SOLDIERS.

NEGROES AS SOLDIERS.

A QUESTION of much importance is presented to our National Government at this time respecting the employment of negroes as soldiers. Those on whom devolves the responsibility of suppressing this monstrous Rebellion, must ultimately, and at no distant day, decide the matter. In their decision, they will undoubtedly be influenced by a regard to the usage and experience, in this respect, of those who directed our military affairs in the war of Independence, as well as by a consideration of the probable effect of their action on our loyal soldiers, and on the armed traitors who are arrayed against them.

It is not strange that the President, on whom, more than on all others, rests the responsibility of taking the final step in this direction, should pause a while to consider the subject in all its bearings, and to allow public opinion to shape itself more distinctly, that his decision, when made, shall have from the Nation a cordial and general support.

Public opinion heretofore has been divided on this question. In one direction, whenever the subject of negro soldiers is mentioned, there is an outcry, as if an atrocious and unheard-of policy were now about to be introduced, — something at variance with the practice of our Revolutionary leaders, and abhorrent to the moral sentiment and the established usage of civilized and Christian warriors.

On the other hand, Governor Sprague of Rhode Island, a conservative of the first degree, but convinced that there is something more worthy of conservation than treacherous timidity or popular prejudice, calls upon the colored people of his own patriotic State to follow the example of their fathers in the war of Seventy-six, and form themselves into a regi-

12

ment, which he proposes, at the proper time, to lead to the field in person.

To throw some light from the history of the past, I propose, by a reference to the annals of the American Revolution and a citation of competent authorities, to exhibit the opinions of the patriot statesmen and soldiers of that period, and their action in regard to negroes as soldiers, as well as the result of their experiment.

Two or three incidents in the earliest conflicts with the British troops will show how little prejudice there was against negroes at the commencement of the war, and how ready the citizens generally then were, not only to secure their services as fellow-soldiers, but to honor them for their patriotism and valor.

In the "Boston Gazette, or Weekly Journal," of Tuesday, Oct. 2, 1750, there was published the following advertisement: —

"RAN-away from his master *William Brown* of *Framingham*, on the 30th of *Sept.* last, a Molatto Fellow, about 27 Years of Age, named *Crispas*, 6 Feet 2 Inches high, short curl'd Hair, his Knees nearer together than common; had on a light colour'd Bearskin Coat, plain brown Fustian Jacket, or brown all-Wool one, new Buckskin Breeches, blue Yarn Stockings, and a checked woolen Shirt.

"Whoever shall take up said Run-away, and convey him to his abovesaid Master, shall have *ten Pounds*, old Tenor Reward, and all necessary Charges paid. And all Masters of Vessels and others, are hereby cautioned against concealing or carrying off said Servant on Penalty of the Law. *Boston, October* 2, 1750."

The "Molatto Fellow," it seems, did not speedily return to his master, notwithstanding the reward which was offered; for, on the 13th and 20th of November, another advertisement, similar to the above, was published in the same Journal.

The next time that his name appeared in a Boston newspaper, twenty years later, it was under very different circumstances. He was no longer a fugitive slave, but a hero and a martyr.

The Boston Massacre, March 5, 1770, may be regarded as Boston Massacre, March 5, 1770. the first act in the drama of the American Revolution. "From that moment," said Daniel Webster, "we may date the severance of the British Empire." The presence of the British soldiers in King Street excited the patriotic indignation of the people. The whole community was stirred, and sage counsellors were deliberating and writing and talking about the public grievances. But it was not for "the wise and prudent" to be the first to *act* against the encroachments of arbitrary power. "A motley rabble of saucy boys, negroes and mulattoes, Irish Teagues, and outlandish Jack tars," (as John Adams described them in his plea in defence of the soldiers,) could not restrain their emotion, or stop to inquire if what they *must do* was according to the letter of any law. Led by Crispus Attucks, the mulatto slave, and shouting, "The way to get rid of these soldiers is to attack the main guard; strike at the root; this is the nest," with more valor than discretion they rushed to King Street, and were fired upon by Captain Preston's Company. Crispus Attucks was the first to fall: he and Samuel Gray and Jonas Caldwell were killed on the spot. Samuel Maverick and Patrick Carr were mortally wounded.

The excitement which followed was intense. The bells of the town were rung. An impromptu town-meeting was held, and an immense assembly was gathered.

Three days after, on the 8th, a public funeral of the mar- Funeral of the Martyrs. tyrs took place. The shops in Boston were closed; and all the bells of Boston and the neighboring towns were rung. It is said that a greater number of persons assembled on this occasion than were ever before gathered on this continent for a similar purpose. The body of Crispus Attucks, the mulatto slave, had been placed in Faneuil Hall, with that of Caldwell; both being strangers in the city. Maverick was buried from his mother's house in Union Street; and Gray, from his brother's in Royal Exchange Lane. The four hearses formed

Boston
Massacre,
March 5,
1770.
a junction in King Street; and there the procession marched in columns six deep, with a long file of coaches belonging to the most distinguished citizens, to the Middle Burying-ground, where the four victims were deposited in one grave; over which a stone was placed with this inscription:—

> "Long as in Freedom's cause the wise contend,
> Dear to your country shall your fame extend;
> While to the world the lettered stone shall tell
> Where Caldwell, Attucks, Gray, and Maverick fell."

The anniversary of this event was publicly commemorated in Boston by an oration and other exercises every year until after our national Independence was achieved, when the Fourth of July was substituted for the Fifth of March as the more proper day for a general celebration. Not only was the event commemorated, but the martyrs who then gave up their lives were remembered and honored. Dr. Joseph Warren, in his Oration in March, 1775, only two months before he showed the sincerity of his sentiments by sealing them with his own precious blood, gave utterance to the following bold and timely words:—

Joseph
Warren.
"That personal freedom is the natural right of every man, and that property, or an exclusive right to dispose of what he has honestly acquired by his own labor, necessarily arises therefrom, are truths which common sense has placed beyond the reach of contradiction. And no man, or body of men, can, without being guilty of flagrant injustice, claim a right to dispose of the persons or acquisitions of any other man, or body of men, unless it can be proved that such a right has arisen from some compact between the parties, in which it has been explicitly and freely granted." — *Oration*, p. 5.

1775,
17th June.
Battle of
Bunker
Hill.
At the battle of Bunker Hill, on the memorable 17th of June, 1775, negro soldiers stood side by side, and fought bravely, with their white brethren. If on the monument which commemorates that event were inscribed the names of those most worthy of honor for their heroic deeds on that day, high up on the shaft, with the names of Warren and Prescott,

we should find that of PETER SALEM, a negro soldier, once a Peter Salem. slave.

Major Pitcairn, of the British Marines, it is well known, fell just as he mounted the redoubt, shouting "The day is ours!" The shot which laid him low was fired by Peter Salem.

Although the shaft does not bear his name, the pencil of the artist has portrayed the scene, the pen of the impartial historian has recorded his achievement, and the voice of the eloquent orator has resounded his valor.

Colonel Trumbull, in his celebrated historic picture of this Colonel Trumbull's battle, introduces conspicuously the colored patriot. At the picture. time of the battle, the artist, then acting as adjutant, was stationed with his regiment in Roxbury, and saw the action from that point. The picture was painted in 1786, when the event was fresh in his mind. It is a significant historical fact, pertinent to our present research, that, among the limited number of figures introduced on the canvas, more than one negro soldier can be distinctly seen.

And here I may venture to publish an extract from a letter written to me recently by Aaron White, Esq., of Thompson, in Connecticut, in answer to an inquiry on this subject: —

"With regard to the black hero of Bunker Hill, I never knew him Aaron White's personally, nor did I ever hear from his lips the story of his achieve- account ments; but I have better authority. About the year 1807, I heard a of Peter Salem. soldier of the Revolution, who was present at the Bunker-Hill battle, relate to my father the story of the death of Major Pitcairn. He said the Major had passed the storm of our fire without, and had mounted the redoubt, when, waving his sword, he commanded, in a loud voice, the 'rebels' to surrender. His sudden appearance and his commanding air at first startled the men immediately before him. They neither answered nor fired; probably not being exactly certain what was next to be done. At this critical moment, a negro soldier stepped forward, and, aiming his musket directly at the major's bosom, blew him through. My informant declared that he was so near, that he distinctly saw the act. The story made quite an impression on my mind.

Account
of Peter
Salem.

I have frequently heard my father relate the story, and have no doubt of its truth. My father, on the day of the battle, was a mere child, and witnessed the battle and the burning of Charlestown from Roxbury Hill, sitting on the shoulders of the Rev. Mr. Jackson, who said to him as he replaced him on the ground, 'Now, boy, do you remember this.' Consequently, after such an injunction, he would necessarily pay particular attention to anecdotes concerning the first and only battle he ever witnessed."

The Rev. William Barry in his excellent "History of Framingham," and the Hon. Emory Washburn in his valuable "History of Leicester," give pretty full accounts of the colored patriot, who acted so important a part on that memorable occasion. Mr. Washburn says,—

Emory
Washburn.

"That shot was undoubtedly fired by Peter; and the death of Major Pitcairn, with its accompanying circumstances, formed one of the most touching incidents of this eventful day. . . . . After the war, he came to Leicester, and continued to reside there till a short time before his death. The history of the town would be incomplete without giving him a place. . . . . . He was born in Framingham, and was held as a slave, probably until he joined the army; whereby, if not before, he became free. This was the case with many of the slaves in Massachusetts, as no slave could be mustered into the army. If the master suffered this to be done, it worked a practical emancipation. Peter served faithfully as a soldier, during the war, in Col. Nixon's regiment. A part of the time, he was the servant of Col. Nixon, and always spoke of him in terms of admiration." — *History of Leicester*, pp. 266, 267, 308.

When the statue of General Joseph Warren was inaugurated on the 17th of June, 1857, the Honorable Edward Everett, in his Address, did not forget to mention the colored patriot, and thus to secure for his act perpetual record. Such an honor far exceeds that of any sculptured stone. Pointing to the obelisk, Mr. Everett said: —

Edward
Everett's
honorable
mention
of Peter
Salem.

" It commemorates no individual man or State. It stands, indeed, on the soil of Massachusetts, where the battle was fought ; but there it stands equally for Connecticut, New Hampshire, and Rhode Island, and the younger sisters of the New-England family, Vermont and

Maine, whose troops shared with ours the dangers and honors of the day. It stands for Prescott and Warren, but not less for Putnam and Stark and Greene. No name adorns the shaft; but ages hence, though our alphabets may become as obscure as those which cover the monuments of Nineveh and Babylon, its uninscribed surface (on which monarchs might be proud to engrave their titles) will perpetuate the memory of the 17th of June. It is the monument of the day, of the event, of the battle of Bunker Hill; of all the brave men who shared its perils, — alike of Prescott and Putnam and Warren, the chiefs of the day, and the colored man, Salem, who is reported to have shot the gallant Pitcairn, as he mounted the parapet. Cold as the clods on which it rests, still as the silent heavens to which it soars, it is yet vocal, eloquent, in their undivided praise." — *Orations and Speeches*, vol. iii. p. 529.

Edward Everett's honorable mention of Peter Salem.

Another colored soldier, who participated in the battle of Bunker Hill, is favorably noticed in a petition to the General Court, signed by some of the principal officers, less than six months after the event. It is printed from the original manuscript in our State Archives.

Salem Poor.

" To the Honorable General Court of the Massachusetts Bay.

" The subscribers beg leave to report to your Honorable House (which we do in justice to the character of so brave a man), that, under our own observation, we declare that a negro man called Salem Poor, of Col. Frye's regiment, Capt. Ames' company, in the late battle at Charlestown, behaved like an experienced officer, as well as an excellent soldier. To set forth particulars of his conduct would be tedious. We would only beg leave to say, in the person of this said negro centres a brave and gallant soldier. The reward due to so great and distinguished a character, we submit to the Congress.

" JONA. BREWER, Col.	ELIPHALET BODWELL., Sgt.
THOMAS NIXON, Lt.-Col.	JOSIAH FOSTER, Lieut.
WM. PRESCOTT, Col°·	EBENR. VARNUM, 2d Lieut.
EPHM· COREY, Lieut.	WM. HUDSON BALLARD, Cpt.
JOSEPH BAKER, Lieut.	WILLIAM SMITH, Cap.
JOSHUA ROW, Lieut.	JOHN MORTON, Sergt. [?]
JONAS RICHARDSON, Capt.	Lieut. RICHARD WELSH.

" CAMBRIDGE, Dec. 5, 1775.

" In Council, Dec. 21, 1775. — Read, and sent down.

" PEREZ MORTON, *Dep'y Sec'y.*"

(MS. Archives of Massachusetts, vol. clxxx. p. 241.)

Here I cannot forbear calling attention to the opinion of one who was a brave soldier, not only in this battle, but from the commencement to the close of the Revolution; and whose name continues to be honored in his children and his children's children in our own city.

Major Lawrence.

"Samuel Lawrence was born in Groton, April 24, 1754; and was, therefore, in his early manhood when our Revolutionary struggle commenced. In common with all the hardy, intelligent, liberty-loving yeomanry of New England, he espoused the cause of the Colonies, and devoted himself to it with a courage that never failed, a constancy that never faltered, till his country had passed 'from impending servitude to acknowledged independence.' At work in the field, ploughing his paternal acres, when the news of the attack upon Concord reached Groton, he immediately unloosed a horse from his team, and, mounting, rode rapidly through Groton and some of the adjoining towns, spreading the alarm, and summoning the militia to assemble. He returned in season to join his own company at the church at Groton, at twelve o'clock; where, after prayer offered by the pastor of the town, they started for Concord, helped to swell that impetuous tide of resistance which drove back the invaders, and slept that night on Cambridge Common, after a forced march of thirty miles, and hot skirmishes with the retreating foe. From that time to the peace of 1783, he was 'a soldier of the Revolution'; and, with the exception of one or two brief visits to his family and friends at Groton, he was in actual service throughout the whole war. He rose to the rank of major, and for a considerable period was attached to Gen. Sullivan's staff as adjutant; an office for which his powerful lungs and sonorous voice, which could be heard throughout a long line of troops, peculiarly fitted him. He was in many of the severest battles of the Revolution.

"At Bunker Hill, where he was slightly wounded, his coat and hat were pierced with the balls of the enemy, and were preserved in the family for many years. At one time he commanded a company whose rank and file were all negroes, of whose courage, military discipline, and fidelity, he always spoke with respect. On one occasion, being out reconnoitring with this company, he got so far in advance of his command, that he was surrounded, and on the point of being made prisoner by the enemy. The men, soon discovering his peril, rushed to his rescue, and fought with the most determined bravery till that rescue was effectually secured. He never forgot this circumstance, and ever after took especial pains to show kindness and hospitality to any individual of the colored race who came near his dwelling." — *Memoir of William Lawrence, by Rev. S. K. Lothrop, D.D.*, pp. 8, 9.

Major Lawrence.

A single passage from Mr. Bancroft's History will give a succinct and clear account of the condition of the army, in respect to colored soldiers, at the time of the battle of Bunker Hill: —

"Nor should history forget to record, that as in the army at Cambridge, so also in this gallant band, the free negroes of the Colony had their representatives. For the right of free negroes to bear arms in the public defence was, at that day, as little disputed in New England as their other rights. They took their place, not in a separate corps, but in the ranks with the white man; and their names may be read on the pension-rolls of the country, side by side with those of other soldiers of the Revolution." — *Bancroft's History of the U. S.*, vol. vii. p. 421.

George Bancroft.

At the commencement of the war, not only were free negroes received into the army, but, in many instances, slaves also stood in the ranks with freemen. The inconsistency, however, in using as soldiers, in an army raised for establishing National Liberty, those who were held in bondage, was too gross for the practice long to continue. This was virtually acknowledged in a Resolution which was adopted before the first great battle had been fought.

On the 20th of May, the Committee of Safety

"*Resolved*, That it is the opinion of this Committee, as the contest now between Great Britain and the Colonies respects the liberties and privileges of the latter, which the Colonies are determined to maintain, that the admission of any persons, as Soldiers, into the Army now raising, but only such as are Freemen, will be inconsistent with the principles that are to be supported, and reflect dishonor on this Colony; and that no Slaves be admitted into this army upon any consideration whatever." — *Force's American Archives*, Fourth Series, vol. ii. p. 762.

Committee of Safety.

13

The celebrated divine, the Rev. Dr. Hopkins of Newport, R. I., soon after the commencement of hostilities, published a "Dialogue concerning the Slavery of the Africans," which he dedicated to "The Honorable Continental Congress." As this tract was re-issued in New York by the Manumission Society, of which Robert R. Livingston, Alexander Hamilton, and John Jay were active members, and a copy of it sent, by their direction, to each member of Congress, the views it contains are quite important as illustrating the sentiment of some of the ablest men of that time. The following extract is from a note to the "Dialogue:"—

Rev. Dr. Hopkins.

"God is so ordering it in his providence, that it seems absolutely necessary something should speedily be done with respect to the slaves among us, in order to our safety, and to prevent their turning against us in our present struggle, in order to get their liberty. Our oppressors have planned to gain the blacks, and induce them to take up arms against us, by promising them liberty on this condition; and this plan they are prosecuting to the utmost of their power, by which means they have persuaded numbers to join them. And should we attempt to restrain them by force and severity, keeping a strict guard over them, and punishing them severely who shall be detected in attempting to join our opposers, this will only be making bad worse, and serve to render our inconsistence, oppression, and cruelty more criminal, perspicuous, and shocking, and bring down the righteous vengeance of Heaven on our heads. The only way pointed out to prevent this threatening evil is to set the blacks at liberty ourselves by some public acts and laws, and then give them proper encouragement to labor, or take arms in the defence of the American cause, as they shall choose. This would at once be doing them some degree of justice, and defeating our enemies in the scheme that they are prosecuting." — *Hopkins's Works*, vol. ii. p. 584.

Many slaves were manumitted that they might become soldiers. They served faithfully to the close of the war. Their skill and bravery were never called in question, but, on the contrary, were frequently commended. There does not, however, appear to have been, at that time, any special

legislation sanctioning the employment of Negroes as soldiers.
Authority was given by the Provincial Congress of South
Carolina, Nov. 20, 1775, for military officers to use slaves for
certain purposes, as will be seen by the following resolution:—

"On motion, *Resolved*, That the colonels of the several regiments South
of militia throughout the Colony have leave to enroll such a num- Provincial
ber of able male slaves, to be employed as pioneers and laborers, as Congress.
public exigencies may require ; and that a daily pay of seven shillings
and sixpence be allowed for the service of each such slave while
actually employed." — *American Archives*, Fourth Series, vol. iv.
p. 61.

This resolution must not be regarded as a general sanction, Unsettled
on the part of South Carolina, of the employment of slaves as respecting
soldiers. Such was far from being the case. Although some soldiers.
of her ablest statesmen and bravest soldiers on several occasions advocated strongly in the Continental Congress, and in
the Provincial Legislature, such a use of Negroes, there
was a strong, successful, and disastrous opposition to the
measure.

The first general order issued by Ward, the commanding
officer, required a return of the "complexion" of the soldiers.
It would be interesting, and not very difficult for any one
who has access to the early rolls of the army, and leisure to
examine them, to ascertain the number of negroes who became soldiers. It would also be interesting, and perhaps not
wholly unprofitable, to trace the progress of opinion on this
subject, from the time when the opposition to negro soldiers
first commenced, until it was so far overcome, that nearly
every State, by legislative act or by practice, sanctioned their
employment. The most that I can do, in this paper, is to
produce some specimens of the opinions, laws, and action of
that period. It may be well to observe, that what has caused
so much complaint in the management of the present civil
war—the apparently vacillating action and unsettled policy

of the administration and the army with regard to the use of negroes as soldiers — is not without a precedent, "an historic parallel," in the annals of the Revolutionary War.

Although slavery existed throughout the country, it is a significant fact, that the principal opposition to negro soldiers came from the States where there was the least hearty and efficient support of the principles of Republican Government, and the least ability or disposition to furnish an equal or fair quota of white soldiers.

South Carolina and Georgia contained so many Tories, at one time, that it was supposed the British officers, who elsewhere would, by proclamation, free all negroes joining the Royal Army, might hesitate to meddle with them in these Colonies, lest "the king's friends" should suffer thereby.

John Adams, in his "Diary," under the date of the 28th of September, 1775, gives an account of an interview with Mr. Bullock and Mr. Houston, of Georgia; in which the following statement occurs : —

Georgia and South Carolina.

"The question was, whether all America was not in a state of war, and whether we ought to confine ourselves to act upon the defensive only? He was for acting offensively next spring or this fall, if the petition was rejected or neglected. If it was not answered, and favorably answered, he would be for acting against Britain and Britons, as, in open war, against French and Frenchmen; fit privateers, and take their ships anywhere. These gentlemen give a melancholy account of the state of Georgia and South Carolina. They say, that if one thousand regular troops should land in Georgia, and their commander be provided with arms and clothes enough, and proclaim freedom to all the negroes who would join his camp, twenty thousand negroes would join it from the two Provinces in a fortnight. The negroes have a wonderful art of communicating intelligence among themselves: it will run several hundreds of miles in a week or fortnight. They say their only security is this: that all the king's friends, and tools of government, have large plantations, and property in negroes; so that the slaves of the Tories would be lost, as well as those of the Whigs." — *Works of John Adams*, vol. ii. p. 428.

On the 10th of July, 1775, there was issued at Cambridge, by General Gates, an order determining what persons were to be excluded by the recruiting officers, who were immediately to go upon that service.

"You are not to enlist any deserter from the Ministerial Army, nor any stroller, negro, or vagabond, or person suspected of being an enemy to the liberty of America, nor any under eighteen years of age. Order concerning enlistments.

"As the cause is the best that can engage men of courage and principle to take up arms, so it is expected that none but such will be accepted by the recruiting officer. The pay, provision, &c., being so ample, it is not doubted but that the officers sent upon this service will, without delay, complete their respective corps, and march the men forthwith to camp.

"You are not to enlist any person who is not an American born, unless such person has a wife and family, and is a settled resident in this country. The persons you enlist must be provided with good and complete arms." — *From Gaines's Mercury*, July 24, (*in Frank Moore's Diary of the American Revolution*, vol. i. p. 110.)

On the 26th of September following, according to Mr. Bancroft, "Edward Rutledge, of South Carolina, moved the discharge of all the negroes in the army, and he was strongly supported by many of the Southern delegates; but the opposition was so powerful and so determined, that 'he lost his point.'" Orders to exclude negroes.

On the 18th of October, a Committee of Conference, consisting of Dr. Franklin, Benjamin Harrison, and Thomas Lynch, met at Cambridge, with the Deputy-Governors of Connecticut and Rhode Island, a Committee of the Council of Massachusetts Bay, and General Washington, to consider the condition of the army, and to devise means for its improvement. On the 23d of October, the subject of negro soldiers came before them for action, and was thus decided: —

"Ought not negroes to be excluded from the new enlistment, especially such as are slaves? All were thought improper by the council of officers.

"*Agreed*, That they be rejected altogether." — *Force's American Archives*, Fourth Series, vol. iii. p. 1161.

The following extract from the Orderly Book, under the date of November 12th, indicates the spirit that prevailed in enlisting the new army : —

" The officers are to be careful not to enlist any person suspected of being unfriendly to the liberties of America, or any abandoned vagabond, to whom all causes and countries are equal and alike indifferent. The rights of mankind and the freedom of America will have numbers sufficient to support them, without resorting to such wretched assistance. Let those who wish to put shackles upon freemen fill their ranks with such miscreants, and place their confidence in them. Neither negroes, boys unable to bear arms, nor old men unfit to endure the fatigues of the campaign, are to be enlisted." — *Sparks's Washington*, vol. iii. p. 155.

Negroes to be enlisted. On the 31st of December, 1775, Washington wrote from Cambridge to the President of Congress in regard to the army, in which he thus alludes to negro soldiers : —

" It has been represented to me, that the free negroes who have served in this army are very much dissatisfied at being discarded. As it is to be apprehended that they may seek employ in the Ministerial Army, I have presumed to depart from the resolution respecting them, and have given license for their being enlisted. If this is disapproved of by Congress, I will put a stop to it." — *Sparks's Washington*, vol. iii. pp. 218, 219.

Mr. Sparks appends to this letter the following note : —

" At a meeting of the general officers, previously to the arrival of the committee from Congress in camp, it was unanimously resolved, that it was not expedient to enlist slaves in the new army ; and, by a large majority, negroes of every description were excluded from enlistment. When the subject was referred to the committee in conference, this decision was confirmed. In regard to free negroes, however, the resolve was not adhered to, and probably for the reason here mentioned by General Washington. Many black soldiers were in the service during all stages of the war." — *Sparks's Washington*, vol. iii. pp. 218, 219.

On the 16th of January, 1776, Congress thus decided the question submitted by Washington:—

"That the free negroes, who have served faithfully in the army at Cambridge, may be re-enlisted therein, but no others." — *Journals of Congress*, vol. ii. p. 26.

An extract from a letter of General Thomas to John Adams gives a true picture of the army by one fully competent to describe it:— Account of the army in 1775.

"I am sorry to hear that any prejudices should take place in any Southern colony, with respect to the troops raised in this. I am certain the insinuations you mention are injurious, if we consider with what precipitation we were obliged to collect an army. In the regiments at Roxbury, the privates are equal to any that I served with in the last war; very few old men, and in the ranks very few boys. Our fifers are many of them boys. We have some negroes; but I look on them, in general, equally serviceable with other men for fatigue; and, in action, many of them have proved themselves brave.

"I would avoid all reflection, or any thing that may tend to give umbrage; but there is in this army from the southward a number called riflemen, who are as indifferent men as I ever served with. These privates are mutinous, and often deserting to the enemy; unwilling for duty of any kind; exceedingly vicious; and, I think, the army here would be as well without as with them. But to do justice to their officers, they are, some of them, likely men." — *MS. Letter*, dated 24th October, 1775.

While the question of employing negroes as soldiers was producing a troublesome controversy in the Army and in Congress, our enemies boldly met the matter in a practical manner. Lord Dunmore, the Royal Governor of Virginia, issued a proclamation in November, 1775, promising freedom to all slaves who would join the army of the British. In a recent "History of England," this act is thus described:— Lord Dunmore's Proclamation.

"In letters which had been laid before the English Parliament, and published to the whole world, he had represented the planters as ambitious, selfish men, pursuing their own interests and advancement at the expense of their poorer countrymen, and as being ready to make every sacrifice of honesty and principle; and he had said more

English
account
of Lord
Dunmore's
action.

privately, that, since they were so anxious for liberty, — for more freedom than was consistent with the free institutions of the mother-country and the charter of the Colony, — that since they were so eager to abolish a fanciful slavery in a dependence on Great Britain, he would try how they liked an abolition of real slavery by setting free all their negroes and indentured servants, who were, in fact, little better than *white* slaves. This, to the Virginians, was like passing a rasp over a gangrened place : it was probing a wound that was incurable, or which has not yet been healed. Later in the year, when the battle of Bunker's Hill had been fought, when our forts on Lake Champlain had been taken from us, and when Montgomery and Arnold were pressing on our possessions in Canada, Lord Dunmore carried his threat into execution. Having established his head-quarters at Norfolk, he proclaimed freedom to all the slaves who would repair to his standard and bear arms for the king. The summons was readily obeyed by most of the negroes who had the means of escaping to him. He, at the same time, issued a proclamation, declaring martial law throughout the Colony of Virginia ; and he collected a number of armed vessels, which cut off the coasting-trade, made many prizes, and greatly distressed an important part of that Province. If he could have opened a road to the slaves in the interior of the Province, his measures would have been very fatal to the planters. In order to stop the alarming desertion of the negroes, and to arrest his Lordship in his career, the Provincial Assembly detached against him a strong force of more than a thousand men, who arrived in the neighborhood of Norfolk in the month of December. Having made a circuit, they came to a village called Great Bridge, where the river Elizabeth was traversed by a bridge ; but, before their arrival, the bridge had been made impassable, and some works, defended chiefly by negroes, had been thrown up." — *Pictorial History of England, George III.*, vol. i. pp. 224, 225.

The Proclamation of Lord Dunmore was as follows : —

Lord
Dunmore's
Proclama-
tion.

" *By his Excellency the Right Honorable* JOHN, *Earl of* DUNMORE, *his Majesty's Lieutenant and Governor-General of the Colony and Dominion of Virginia, and Vice-Admiral of the same,* —

" A PROCLAMATION.

" As I have ever entertained hopes that an accommodation might have taken place between Great Britain and this Colony, without being compelled by my duty to this most disagreeable but now absolutely necessary step, rendered so by a body of armed men, unlawfully assembled, firing on his Majesty's tenders; and the formation of an army, and that army now on their march to attack his Majesty's troops, and destroy the well-disposed subjects of this Colony, — to defeat such treasonable purposes, and that all such traitors and their abettors may be brought to justice, and that the peace and good order of this Colony may be again restored, which the ordinary course of the civil law is unable to effect, I have thought fit to issue this my Proclamation; hereby declaring, that, until the aforesaid good purposes can be obtained, I do, in virtue of the power and authority to me given by his Majesty, determine to execute martial law, and cause the same to be executed, throughout this Colony. And, to the end that peace and good order may the sooner be restored, I do require every person capable of bearing arms to resort to his Majesty's standard, or be looked upon as traitors to his Majesty's Crown and Government, and thereby become liable to the penalty the law inflicts upon such offences, — such as forfeiture of life, confiscation of lands, &c., &c. And I do hereby further declare all indented servants, negroes, or others, (appertaining to rebels,) free, that are able and willing to bear arms, they joining his Majesty's troops, as soon as may be, for the more speedily reducing this Colony to a proper sense of their duty to his Majesty's crown and dignity. I do further order and require all his Majesty's liege subjects to retain their quit-rents, or any other taxes due, or that may become due, in their own custody, till such time as peace may be again restored to this at present most unhappy country, or demanded of them, for their former salutary purposes, by officers properly authorized to receive the same.

"Given under my hand, on board the ship 'William,' off Norfolk, the seventh day of November, in the sixteenth year of his Majesty's reign.   "DUNMORE.
"*God save the King!*"

(Force's "American Archives," Fourth Series, vol. iii. p. 1385.)

This Proclamation created great consternation in Virginia. It will be seen by the following extract from a letter written November 27th, 1775, by Edmund Pendleton to Richard Henry Lee, that many slaves flocked to the British standard.

Letter from
Edmund
Pendleton
to Richard
Henry Lee,
Nov. 27,
1775.
"The Governor, hearing of this, marched out with three hundred and fifty soldiers, Tories and slaves, to Kemp's Landing; and after setting up his standard, and issuing his proclamation, declaring all persons rebels who took up arms for the country, and inviting all slaves, servants, and apprentices to come to him and receive arms, he proceeded to intercept Hutchings and his party, upon whom he came by surprise, but received, it seems, so warm a fire, that the ragamuffins gave way. They were, however, rallied on discovering that two companies of our militia gave way; and left Hutchings and Dr. Reid with a volunteer company, who maintained their ground bravely till they were overcome by numbers, and took shelter in a swamp. The slaves were sent in pursuit of them; and one of Col. Hutchings's own, with another, found him. On their approach, he discharged his pistol at his slave, but missed him; and was taken by them, after receiving a wound in his face with a sword. The numbers taken or killed, on either side, is not ascertained. It is said the Governor went to Dr. Reid's shop, and, after taking the medicines and dressings necessary for his wounded men, broke all the others to pieces. Letters mention that slaves flock to him in abundance; but I hope it is magnified." — *Force's American Archives*, Fourth Series, vol. iv. p. 202.

In a paper published in Williamsburg, Virginia, on the 23d of November, the Proclamation is severely commented on; and an urgent appeal is made to the negroes to stand by their masters, — their true friends, — who would, " were it in their power, restore freedom to such as have unhappily lost it."

Caution
to the
negroes.
" 'The second class of people for whose sake a few remarks upon this proclamation seem necessary is the negroes. They have been flattered with their freedom, if they be able to bear arms, and will speedily join Lord Dunmore's troops. To none, then, is freedom promised, but to such as are able to do Lord Dunmore service. The aged, the infirm, the women and children, are still to remain the property of their masters, — of masters who will be provoked to severity, should part of their slaves desert them. Lord Dunmore's declaration, therefore, is a cruel declaration to the negroes. He does not pretend to make it out of any tenderness to them, but solely upon his own account; and, should it meet with success, it leaves by far

the greater number at the mercy of an enraged and injured people. Appeal to the negroes But should there be any amongst the negroes weak enough to believe by their that Lord Dunmore intends to do them a kindness, and wicked enough masters. to provoke the fury of the Americans against their defenceless fathers and mothers, their wives, their women and children, let them only consider the difficulty of effecting their escape, and what they must expect to suffer if they fall into the hands of the Americans. Let them further consider what must be their fate should the English prove conquerors. If we can judge of the future from the past, it will not be much mended. Long have the Americans, moved by compassion and actuated by sound policy, endeavored to stop the progress of slavery. Our Assemblies have repeatedly passed acts, laying heavy duties upon imported negroes; by which they meant altogether to prevent the horrid traffic. But their humane intentions have been as often frustrated by the cruelty and covetousness of a set of English merchants, who prevailed upon the King to repeal our kind and merciful acts, little, indeed, to the credit of his humanity. Can it, then, be supposed that the negroes will be better used by the English, who have always encouraged and upheld this slavery, than by their present masters, who pity their condition; who wish, in general, to make it as easy and comfortable as possible; *and who would, were it in their power, or were they permitted, not only prevent any more negroes from losing their freedom, but restore it to such as have already unhappily lost it?* No: the ends of Lord Dunmore and his party being answered, they will either give up the offending negroes to the rigor of the laws they have broken, or sell them in the West Indies, where every year they sell many thousands of their miserable brethren, to perish either by the inclemency of weather or the cruelty of barbarous masters. Be not then, ye negroes, tempted by this proclamation to ruin yourselves. I have given you a faithful view of what you are to expect; and declare before God, in doing it, I have considered your welfare, as well as that of the country. Whether you will profit by my advice, I cannot tell; but this I know, that, whether we suffer or not, if *you* desert us, *you* most certainly will." — *Force's American Archives*, Fourth Series, vol. iii. p. 1387.

The Virginia Convention appointed a Committee to prepare a Declaration in answer to Lord Dunmore's Proclamation. This was adopted on the 13th of December, when the same Committee was instructed to report another Declaration,

Declaration of pardon to slaves. " offering pardon to such slaves as shall return to their duty within ten days after the publication thereof." This also was adopted the next day, in the following terms:—

" *By the Representatives of the People of the Colony and Dominion of Virginia, assembled in General Convention,*

" A DECLARATION.

" Whereas Lord Dunmore, by his Proclamation dated on board the ship ' William,' off Norfolk, the seventh day of November, 1775, hath offered feeedom to such able-bodied slaves as are willing to join him, and take up arms against the good people of this Colony, giving thereby encouragement to a general insurrection, which may induce a necessity of inflicting the severest punishments upon those unhappy people, already deluded by his base and insidious arts; and whereas, by an act of the General Assembly now in force in this Colony, it is enacted, that all negro or other slaves, conspiring to rebel or make insurrection, shall suffer death, and be excluded all benefit of clergy; — we think it proper to declare, that all slaves who have been or shall be seduced, by his Lordship's Proclamation, or other arts, to desert their masters' service, and take up arms against the inhabitants of this Colony, shall be liable to such punishment as shall hereafter be directed by the General Convention. And to the end that all such who have taken this unlawful and wicked step may return in safety to their duty, and escape the punishment due to their crimes, we hereby promise pardon to them, they surrendering themselves to Colonel William Woodford or any other commander of our troops, and not appearing in arms after the publication hereof. And we do further earnestly recommend it to all humane and benevolent persons in this Colony to explain and make known this our offer of mercy to those unfortunate people." — *Force's American Archives,* Fourth Series, vol. iv. pp. 84, 85.

Washington saw what an element of strength Lord Dunmore had called to his aid, and the importance of acting promptly and with energy against him. On the 15th of December, he thus wrote to Joseph Reed:—

Lord Dunmore to be crushed. " If the Virginians are wise, that arch-traitor to the rights of humanity, Lord Dunmore, should be instantly crushed, if it takes the force of the whole army to do it; otherwise, like a snow-ball in

rolling, his army will get size, some through fear, some through Lord Dunmore.
promises, and some through inclination, joining his standard: but
that which renders the measure indispensably necessary is the negroes; for, if he gets formidable, numbers of them will be tempted
to join who will be afraid to do it without." — *Life and Correspondence of Joseph Reed*, vol. i. 135.

Although many of the slaves responded to the proclamation
by joining the army of the enemy, the greater part of them
were too shrewd to be caught by such wily arts. They were
unwilling to trust their freedom to the officers of a government which had persistently encouraged the slave-trade
against the remonstrances of their masters, who had not only
declared that traffic to be a wrong against humanity, but had
expressed their desire to abolish domestic slavery as soon as
it was practicable for them to do so. The inconsistency and
atrocity of Lord Dunmore's conduct justly met with very
general indignation. Subsequent events proved that the
distrust and fears, felt by the slaves, were well founded.

It will be seen by letters written several months after
the Proclamation was issued, that his Lordship attributed the
limited success which attended it to another than the true
cause.

" *Lord Dunmore to the Secretary of State.*

" [No. 1.]   " SHIP 'DUNMORE,' IN ELIZABETH RIVER, VA.,
                                30th March, 1776.

" Your Lordship will observe by my letter, No. 34, that I have
been endeavoring to raise two regiments here, — one of white people,
the other of black. The former goes on very slowly; but the latter
very well, and would have been in great forwardness, had not a fever
crept in amongst them, which carried off a great many very fine
fellows."

" [No. 3.]   " SHIP 'DUNMORE,' IN GWIN'S ISLAND HARBOR, VA.,
                                June 26, 1776.

" I am extremely sorry to inform your Lordship, that that fever,
of which I informed you in my letter No. 1, has proved a very ma-
lignant one, and has carried off an incredible number of our people,

especially the blacks. Had it not been for this horrid disorder, I am
satisfied I should have had two thousand blacks ; with whom I should
have had no doubt of penetrating into the heart of this Colony."

(Force's " American Archives," Fifth Series, vol. ii. pp. 160, 162.)

Negro
Soldiers.

During the years 1776 and 1777, not much was done by
way of legislation towards settling a general policy with regard to the employment of negroes as soldiers. They continued, in fact, to be admitted into the line of the army without
much objection.

A letter from General Greene to Washington shows that it
was then contemplated to form the negroes at Staten Island
into an independent regiment.

"CAMP ON LONG ISLAND,
July 21, 1776, two o'clock.

" SIR, — Colonel Hand reports seven large ships are coming up
from the Hook to the Narrows.

" A negro belonging to one Strickler, at Gravesend, was taken
prisoner (as he says) last Sunday at Concy Island. Yesterday he
made his escape, and was taken prisoner by the rifle-guard. He reports eight hundred negroes collected on Staten Island, this day to be
formed into a regiment.

" I am your Excellency's most obedient, humble servant,
" N. GREENE.
" To his Excellency Gen. WASHINGTON, Head-quarters, New York."

(Force's " American Archives," Fifth Series, vol. i. p. 486.)

Negro
Prisoners.

A Resolve of the Massachusetts Legislature, in September,
1776, is worthy of special notice. Referring to it, a writer
in the " Historical Magazine " for September, 1861, says,
" The course of the authorities of the Southern States, now in
arms against the Government, in selling as slaves all negroes
taken prisoners, is the last relic of a barbarous custom. . . .
The first condemnation of the course seems to be that contained in a Massachusetts Resolve, of the 14th of September,
1776, forbidding the sale, as slaves, of two negroes taken on
the sloop ' Hannibal.' " The Resolve is as follows : —

"Whereas this Court is credibly informed, that two negro men lately taken on the high seas, on board the sloop 'Hannibal,' and brought into this State as prisoners, are advertised to be sold at Salem the 17th instant, by public auction: Negroes to be treated like other prisoners of war.

"*Resolved*, That all persons concerned with the said negroes be, and they hereby are, forbidden to sell them, or in any manner to treat them otherwise than is already ordered for the treatment of prisoners taken in like manner; and, if any sale of the said negroes shall be made, it is hereby declared null and void. And that whenever it shall appear that any negroes are taken on the high seas, and brought as prisoners into this State, they shall not be allowed to be sold, nor treated any otherwise than as prisoners are ordered to be treated who are taken in like manner." — *Resolves, September*, 1776, p. 14.

I am indebted to my friend Mr. William J. Davis, of New York, for the following extract from the Journal of a Hessian officer who was with Burgoyne at the time of his surrender. It is a literal translation from a German work which is rare in this country. This testimony of a foreign officer, as to the common use of negroes in the American Army, is quite important. It is dated 23d October, 1777.

"From here to Springfield, there are few habitations which have not a negro family dwelling in a small house near by. The negroes are here as fruitful as other cattle. The young ones are well foddered, especially while they are still calves. Slavery is, moreover, very gainful. The negro is to be considered just as the bond-servant of a peasant. The negress does all the coarse work of the house, and the little black young ones wait on the little white young ones. *The negro can take the field, instead of his master; and therefore no regiment is to be seen in which there are not negroes in abundance: and among them there are able-bodied, strong, and brave fellows.* Here, too, there are many families of free negroes, who live in good houses, have property, and live just like the rest of the inhabitants." — *Schloezer's Briefwechsel*, vol. iv. p. 365. Hessian officer's testimony.

The capture of Major-General Prescott, of the British army, on the 9th of July, 1777, was an occasion of great joy throughout the country. Prince, the valiant negro who seized that officer, ought always to be remembered with honor

Capture of the British General Prescott. for his important service. The exploit was much commended at the time, as its results were highly important; and Colonel Barton, very properly, received from Congress the compliment of a sword for his ingenuity and bravery. It seems, however, that it took more than one head to plan and to execute the undertaking.

"They landed about five miles from Newport, and three-quarters of a mile from the house, which they approached cautiously, avoiding the main guard, which was at some distance. *The Colonel went foremost, with a stout, active negro close behind him, and another at a small distance: the rest followed so as to be near, but not seen.*

"A single sentinel at the door saw and hailed the Colonel: he answered by exclaiming against, and inquiring for, rebel prisoners, but kept slowly advancing. The sentinel again challenged him, and required the countersign. He said he had not the countersign; but amused the sentry by talking about rebel prisoners, and still advancing till he came within reach of the bayonet, which, he presenting, the colonel suddenly struck aside, and seized him. He was immediately secured, and ordered to be silent, on pain of instant death. *Meanwhile, the rest of the men surrounding the house, the negro, with his head, at the second stroke, forced a passage into it, and then into the landlord's apartment. The landlord at first refused to give the necessary intelligence; but, on the prospect of present death, he pointed to the General's chamber, which being instantly opened by the negro's head, the Colonel, calling the General by name, told him he was a prisoner.*" — *Pennsylvania Evening Post*, Aug. 7, 1777; (in *Frank Moore's Diary of the American Revolution*, vol. i. p. 468.)

The event was thus noticed by a contemporary (Dr. Thacher), who was a surgeon in the American army: —

Doctor Thacher's account. "*Albany*, Aug. 3, 1777. — The pleasing information is received here that Lieut.-Col. Barton, of the Rhode-Island militia, planned a bold exploit for the purpose of surprising and taking Major-Gen. Prescott, the commanding officer of the royal army at Newport. Taking with him, in the night, about forty men, in two boats, with oars muffled, he had the address to elude the vigilance of the ships-of-war and guard-boats: and, having arrived undiscovered at the quarters of Gen. Prescott, they were taken for the sentinels; and the general was not alarmed till his captors were at the door of his lodging-chamber, which was fast closed. *A negro man, named Prince, instantly thrust his beetle head through the panel door, and seized his victim while in bed.* . . . This event is extremely honorable to the enterprising spirit of Col. Barton, and is considered as ample retaliation for the capture of Gen. Lee by Col. Harcourt. The event occasions great joy and exultation, as it puts in our possession an officer of equal rank with Gen. Lee, by which means an exchange may be obtained. Congress resolved that an elegant sword should be presented to Col. Barton for his brave exploit." Doctor Thacher's account.

It was perhaps "Prince" to whom Dr. Thacher alludes in the following characteristic anecdote: —

"When the Count D'Estaing's fleet appeared near the British batteries, in the harbor of Rhode Island, a severe cannonade was commenced; and several shot passed through the houses in town, and occasioned great consternation among the inhabitants. A shot passed through the door of Mrs. Mason's house, just above the floor. The family were alarmed, not knowing where to flee for safety. A negro man ran and sat himself down very composedly, with his back against the shot-hole in the door; and, being asked by young Mr. Mason why he chose that situation, he replied, 'Massa, you never know two bullet go in one place.'" — *Thacher's Military Journal, pp. 87, 175.*

The subject of the employment of Negro soldiers came before the Connecticut General Assembly in 1777, in connection with the subject of slavery and emancipation.

By the courtesy of J. Hammond Trumbull, Esquire, Editor of "The Public Records of the Colony of Connecticut," and Secretary of State, I am enabled to give, in his own words, the following interesting account of the action of that State: —

"In May, 1777, the General Assembly of Connecticut appointed a Committee ' to take into consideration the state and condition of the negro and mulatto slaves in this State, and what may be done for their emancipation.' This Committee, in a report presented at the same session (signed by the chairman, the Hon. Matthew Griswold of Lyme), recommended — Action of the Connecticut Assembly.

15

" ' That the effective negro and mulatto slaves be allowed to enlist
with the Continental battalions now raising in this State, under the
following regulations and restrictions: viz., that all such negro and
mulatto slaves as can procure, either by bounty, hire, or in any other
way, such a sum to be paid to their masters as such negro or mulatto
shall be judged to be reasonably worth by the selectmen of the town
where such negro or mulatto belongs, shall be allowed to enlist into
either of said battalions, and shall thereupon be, de facto, *free and
emancipated;* and that the master of such negro or mulatto shall be
exempted from the support and maintenance of such negro or mulatto,
in case such negro or mulatto shall hereafter become unable to support and maintain himself.

" ' And that, in case any such negro or mulatto slave shall be
disposed to enlist into either of said battalions during the [war], he
shall be allowed so to do: and such negro or mulatto shall be
appraised by the selectmen of the town to which he belongs; and his
master shall be allowed to receive the bounty to which such slave
may be entitled, and also one-half of the annual wages of such slave
during the time he shall continue in said service; provided, however,
that said master shall not be allowed to receive such part of said
wages after he shall have received so much as amounts, together with
the bounty, to the sum at which he was appraised.' "

This report, in the Lower House, was ordered to be continued to the next session of the Assembly. In the Upper
House it was rejected.

Mr. Trumbull writes:—

" You will see by the Report of Committee, May, 1777, that General Varnum's plan for the enlistment of slaves had been anticipated
in Connecticut; with this difference, that Rhode Island *adopted* it,
while Connecticut did *not.*

" The two States reached nearly the same *results* by different
methods. The unanimous declaration of the officers at Cambridge,
in the winter of 1775, *against* the enlistment of slaves,—confirmed
by the Committee of Congress,—had some weight, I think, with the
Connecticut Assembly, so far as the formal enactment of a law
authorizing such enlistments was in question. At the same time,
Washington's license to *continue* the enlistment of negroes was regarded as a rule of action, both by the selectmen in making up, and by

the State Government in accepting, the quota of the towns. The Legislation process of draughting, in Connecticut, was briefly this: The able-bodied men, in each town, were divided into 'classes'; and each class was required to furnish one or more men, as the town's quota required, to answer a draught. Now, the Assembly, at the same session at which the proposition for enlisting slaves was rejected (May, 1777), passed an act providing that any *two* men belonging to this State, 'who should procure an able-bodied soldier or recruit to enlist into either of the Continental battalions to be raised from this State,' should themselves be exempted from draught during the continuance of such enlistment. Of recruits or draughted men thus furnished, neither the selectmen nor commanding officers questioned the *color* or the civil *status:* white and black, bond and free, if 'able-bodied,' went on the roll together, accepted as the representatives of their 'class,' or as substitutes for their employers. At the next session (October, 1777), an act was passed which gave more direct encouragement to the enlistment of slaves. By the existing law, the master who emancipated a slave was not released from the liability to provide for his support. This law was now so amended, as to authorize the selectmen of any town, on the application of the master,—after 'inquiry into the age, abilities, circumstances, and character' of the servant or slave, and being satisfied 'that it was likely to be consistent with his real advantage, and that it was probable that he would be able to support himself,'—to grant liberty for his emancipation, and to discharge the master 'from any charge or cost which may be occasioned by maintaining or supporting the servant or slave made free as aforesaid.' This enactment enabled the selectmen to offer an additional inducement to enlistment, for making up the quota of the town. The slave (or servant for term of years) might receive his freedom: the master might secure exemption from draught, and a discharge from future liabilities, to which he must otherwise have been subjected. In point of fact, some hundreds of blacks — slaves and freemen — were enlisted, from time to time, in the regiments of the State troops and of the Connecticut line. *How* many, it is impossible to tell; for, from first to last, the company or regimental rolls indicate *no distinctions* of color. The *name* is the only guide: and, in turning over the rolls of the Connecticut line, the frequent recurrence of names which were exclusively appropriated to negroes and slaves, shows how considerable was their proportion of the material of the Connecticut army; while such surnames as ' Liberty,'

Legislation in Connecticut.

Legislation in Connecticut. 'Freeman,' 'Freedom,' &c., by scores, indicate with what anticipations, and under what inducements, they entered the service.

"As to the efficiency of the service they rendered, I can say nothing from the records, except what is to be gleaned from scattered files, such as one of the petitions I send you. So far as my acquaintance extends, almost every family has its traditions of the good and faithful service of a black servant or slave, who was killed in battle, or served through the war, and came home to tell stories of hard fighting, and draw his pension. In my own native town, — not a large one, — I remember five such pensioners, three of whom, I believe, had been slaves, and, in fact, *were* slaves to the day of their death; for (and this explains the uniform action of the General Assembly on petitions for emancipation) neither the towns nor the State were inclined to exonerate the master, at a time when slavery was becoming unprofitable, from the obligation to provide for the old age of his slave.

.   .   .   .   .

"Col. William Browne of Salem (a "mandamus counsellor"), who went with the enemy from Boston in 1776, owned large tracts of land in New London and Hartford counties in Connecticut, entailed by his grandfather, Col. Samuel Browne. The General Court cut off the entail, and confiscated the land. A farm in Lyme of twelve thousand four hundred and thirty-six acres, valued, in 1779, at a hundred and sixty-nine thousand pounds (Continental), had been leased for a term of years, with nine *slaves*. The administrator on confiscated estates, Benjamin Huntington, Esq., when returning the inventory of Mr. Browne's property, stated to the General Assembly that there were 'a number of slaves appraised, who beg for their liberty;' and that the lessee of the farm would assent to their being liberated, without requiring a diminution of his rent.

"Accompanying the inventory is the following petition, in Mr. Huntington's hand-writing: —

"'*To the Hon. General Assembly of the State of Connecticut, now sitting in Hartford.*

Petition of loyal slaves. "'The memorial of Great Prince, Little Prince, Luke, Cæsar, and Prue and her three children, — all friends to America, but *slaves* (lately belonging to Col. William Browne, now forfeited to this State,) — humbly sheweth, that their late master was a Tory, and fled from his native country to *his* master, King George; where he now lives like a poor slave.

"'That your memorialists, though they have flat noses, crooked shins, and other queerness of make, peculiar to Africans, are yet of the human race, free-born in our own country, taken from thence by man-stealers, and sold in this country as cattle in the market, without the least act of our own to forfeit liberty; but we hope our good mistress, *the free State of Connecticut*, engaged in a war with tyranny, will not sell good honest Whigs and friends of the freedom and independence of America, as we are, to raise cash to support the war: because the Whigs ought to be *free;* and the *Tories* should be sold.

"' Wherefore your memorialists pray your Honors to consider their case, and grant them their freedom upon their getting security to indemnify the State from any expense for their support in case of want, or in some other way release them from slavery.

"'And your poor negroes, as in duty bound, shall ever pray.

"' GREAT PRINCE.

LITTLE PRINCE.

LUKE, &c.

"'Dated in LYME, Election-day, 1779.'

"The Lower House *granted*, but the Upper House *negatived*, the prayer of the memorial. A committee of conference was appointed; but each House adhered to its original vote."

Nowhere in the country was the question of negro soldiers more carefully considered, or the practice of employing them more generally adopted, than in Rhode Island. Not only were the names of colored men entered with those of white citizens on the rolls of the militia, but a distinct regiment of this class of persons was formed. The character and conduct of that regiment have an important place in the history of the Revolutionary War.

My valued friend, John Russell Bartlett, Esquire, Editor of the "Records of the Colony of Rhode Island and Providence Plantations in New England," and Secretary of State, has copied for me, from the manuscripts in the State Archives, the correspondence and legislation relating to the subject. These documents are here presented entire, and give a full history of the whole matter.

GENERAL WASHINGTON TO GOVERNOR COOKE.

"HEAD QUARTERS, 2d January, 1778.

" SIR, — Enclosed you will receive a copy of a letter from General Varnum to me, upon the means which might be adopted for completing the Rhode-Island troops to their full proportion in the Continental Army.   I have nothing to say, in addition to what I wrote on the 29th of last month, on this important subject, but to desire that you will give the officers employed in this business all the assistance in your power.

" I am, with great respect, Sir, your most obedient servant,

"His Excellency NICHOLAS COOKE, Esq.,   " GEO. WASHINGTON.
    Governor of Rhode Island."

GENERAL VARNUM TO GENERAL WASHINGTON.

"CAMP, Jan. 2, 1778.

" SIR, — The two battalions from the State of Rhode Island being small, and there being a necessity of the State's furnishing an additional number to make up their proportion in the Continental Army, the field-officers have represented to me the propriety of making one temporary battalion from the two ; so that one entire corps of officers may repair to Rhode Island, in order to receive and prepare the recruits for the field.   It is imagined that a battalion of negroes can be easily raised there.   Should that measure be adopted, or recruits obtained upon any other principle, the service will be advanced.   The field-officers who go upon this command are Colonel Greene, Lieut.-Colonel Olney, and Major Ward ; seven captains, twelve lieutenants, six ensigns, one paymaster, one surgeon and mate, one adjutant, and one chaplain.

" I am your Excellency's most obedient servant,

                                                "J. M. VARNUM.
" His Excellency Gen. WASHINGTON."

These letters were laid before the General Assembly at the February session ; and, after due deliberation, the following act was passed, not without some opposition : —

" *State of Rhode Island and Providence Plantations, in General
    Assembly.   February Session,* 1778.

" Whereas, for the preservation of the rights and liberties of the United States, it is necessary that the whole powers of Government should be exerted in recruiting the Continental battalions; and whereas His Excellency Gen. Washington hath inclosed to this State a proposal made to him by Brigadier-General Varnum, to enlist into the two battalions, raising by this State, such slaves as should be willing to enter into the service : and whereas history affords us frequent Precedents of the *wisest*, the *freest*, and *bravest* nations having liberated their Slaves, and inlisted them as Soldiers to fight in Defence of their Country ; and also, whereas, the Enemy, with a great force, have taken Possession of the Capital and of a great Part of this State ; and this State is obliged to raise a very considerable Number of Troops for its own immediate Defence, whereby it is in a Manner rendered impossible for this State to furnish Recruits for the said two Battalions without adopting the said Measure so recommended :

Negro Regiment in Rhode Island.

" *It is Voted and Resolved*, That every able-bodied *negro*, mulatto, or *Indian* man slave, in this State, may inlist into either of the said two battalions to serve during the continuance of the present war with Great Britain : that every slave so inlisting shall be entitled to and receive all the bounties, wages, and encouragements allowed by the Continental Congress to any soldier inlisting into their service.

" *It is further Voted and Resolved*, That every slave so inlisting shall, upon his passing muster before Col. Christopher Greene, be immediately discharged from the service of his master or mistress, and be absolutely FREE, as though he had never been incumbered with any kind of servitude or slavery. And in case such slave shall, by sickness or otherwise, be rendered unable to maintain himself, he shall not be chargeable to his master or mistress, but shall be supported at the expense of the State.

" And whereas slaves have been by the laws deemed the property of their owners ; and therefore compensation ought to be made to the owners for the loss of their service, —

" *It is further Voted and Resolved*, That there be allowed, and paid by this State to the owner, for every such slave so inlisting, a sum according to his worth ; at a price not exceeding one hundred and twenty pounds for the most valuable slave, and in proportion for a slave of less value : *Provided* the owner of said slave shall deliver up to the officer who shall inlist him the clothes of the said slave ; or otherwise he shall not be entitled to said sum.

" And for settling and ascertaining the value of such slaves, —

" *It is further Voted and Resolved*, That a committee of five be appointed, *to wit :* one from each county ; any three of whom to be a quorum, to examine the slaves who shall be so inlisted, after they shall have passed muster, and to set a price upon each slave according to his value, as aforesaid.

"*It is further Voted and Resolved*, That upon any able-bodied *negro*, mulatto, or *Indian* slave, inlisting as aforesaid, the officer who shall so inlist him, after he has passed muster as aforesaid, shall deliver a certificate thereof to the master or mistress of said *negro*, mulatto, or *Indian* slave ; which shall discharge him from the service of said master or mistress as aforesaid.

"*It is further Voted and Resolved*, That the committee who shall estimate the value of any slave as aforesaid, shall give a certificate of the sum at which he may be valued, to the owner of said slave : and the General Treasurer of this State is hereby empowered and directed to give unto the owner of said slave his promissory note, as Treasurer, as aforesaid, for the sum of money at which he shall be valued as aforesaid, payable on demand, with interest, at the rate of six per cent. per annum ; and that said notes which shall be so given, shall be paid with the money which is due this State, and is expected from Congress, — the money which has been borrowed out of the General Treasury by this Assembly being first replaced."

The members of the General Assembly opposed to the passage of this Act embodied their objections to it in a Protest. The difficulties which they apprehended were not found to exist to such an extent as to defeat the project.

"*Protest against enlisting Slaves to serve in the Army.*

"We, the subscribers, beg leave to dissent from the vote of the Lower House ordering a regiment of negroes to be raised for the Continental service, for the following reasons ; viz.

"1st, Because, in our opinion, there is not a sufficient number of negroes in the State who would have an inclination to inlist, and would pass muster, to constitute a regiment ; and raising several companies of blacks would not answer the purposes intended : and therefore the attempt to constitute said regiment would prove abortive, and be a fruitless expense to the State.

"2d, The raising such a regiment upon the footing proposed would suggest an idea, and produce an opinion in the world, that the

State had purchased a band of slaves to be employed in the defence of the rights and liberties of our country : which is wholly inconsistent with those principles of liberty and constitutional government for which we are so ardently contending ; and would be looked upon by the neighboring States in a contemptible point of view, and not equal to their troops ; and they would, therefore, be unwilling that we should have credit for them as for an equal number of white troops ; and would also give occasion to our enemies to suspect that we are not able to procure our own people to oppose them in the field, and to retort upon us the same kind of ridicule we so liberally bestowed upon them on account of Dunmore's regiment of blacks ; or possibly might suggest to them the idea of employing black regiments against us.

" 3d, The expense of purchasing and inlisting said regiment, in the manner proposed, will vastly exceed the expenses of raising an equal number of white men ; and, at the same time, will not have the like good effect.

" 4th, Great difficulties and uneasiness will arise in purchasing the negroes from their masters; and many of the masters will not be satisfied with any prices allowed.

" JOHN NORTHUP.   GEORGE PEIRCE.
JAMES BABCOCK, Jr.   SYLVESTER GARDNER.
OTHNIEL GORTON.   SAMUEL BABCOCK."

THE GOVERNOR OF RHODE ISLAND TO GEN. WASHINGTON.

" PROVIDENCE, Feb. 23, 1778.

" SIR, — I have been favored with your Excellency's letter of the third instant [2d ultimo ?], enclosing a proposal made to you by General Varnum for recruiting the two Continental battalions raised by this State.

" I laid the letter before the General Assembly at their session, on the second Monday in this month ; who, considering the pressing necessity of filling up the Continental Army, and the peculiarly difficult circumstances of this State, — which rendered it, in a manner, impossible to recruit our battalions in any other way, — adopted the measure.

" Liberty is given to every effective slave to enter the service during the war ; and, upon his passing muster, he is absolutely made free, and entitled to all the wages, bounties, and encouragements given by Congress to any soldier enlisting into their service. The masters are allowed at the rate of £120 for the most valuable slave, and in proportion to those of less value.

"The number of slaves in this State is not great; but it is generally thought that three hundred and upwards will be enlisted.

"I am, with great respect, Sir, your Excellency's most obedient, humble servant, "NICHOLAS COOKE.

"To Gen. WASHINGTON."

At the session of the General Assembly in which the Act was passed,—

"It is *voted and resolved*, That Messrs. Thomas Rumreil, Christopher Lippitt, Samuel Babcock, Thomas Tillinghast, and Josiah Humphrey, be, and they are hereby, appointed a committee to estimate the value of the slaves who may enlist into the Continental battalions, agreeably to a resolve of this Assembly."

A short time after the act was passed, March the 9th,—

"It is *voted and resolved*, That the masters of all negro slaves, who are bound out as apprentices, that already have inlisted or shall inlist into the Continental service, shall be entitled to receive out of the General Treasury the annual interest of the sum the said slaves shall be appraised at, until the expiration of their apprenticeships; and that the money remain in the treasury until the expiration of the said apprenticeships, and then be paid to the owner without interest."

As it was not desirable to extend indefinitely the offer of freedom to slaves enlisting under this act, the General Assembly, at their May Session, adopted the following preamble and resolution:—

"Whereas, by an act of this Assembly, negro, mulatto, and Indian slaves, belonging to the inhabitants of this State, are permitted to inlist into the Continental battalions ordered to be raised by this State, and are thereupon for ever manumitted and discharged from the service of their masters; and whereas it is necessary, for answering the purposes intended by the said act, that the same shall be temporary,—

"It is *therefore voted and resolved*, that no negro, mulatto, or Indian slave, be permitted to inlist into said battalions from and after the tenth day of June next; and that the said act then expire, and be no longer in force, any thing therein to the contrary notwithstanding."

At the October Session, 1778, —

Negro soldiers in Rhode Island.

"It is *voted and resolved*, That the General Treasurer pay unto the owners of slaves who have enlisted as aforesaid, and who have not received notes for the estimated value of the same, the sums of money at which they were appraised, upon their producing certificates thereof from the committee appointed to give the same ; and that the said owners be permitted to receive the whole or any part of the value of their slaves in Continental loan-office certificates."

There is abundant evidence of the fidelity and bravery of the colored patriots of Rhode Island during the whole war. Before they had been formed into a separate regiment, they had fought valiantly with the white soldiers at Red Bank and elsewhere. Their conduct at the "Battle of Rhode Island," on the 29th of August, 1778, entitles them to perpetual honor. That battle has been pronounced by military authorities to have been one of the best fought battles of the Revolutionary War. Its success was owing, in a great degree, to the good fighting of the Negro soldiers. Mr. Arnold, in his "History of Rhode Island," thus closes his account of it : —

"A third time the enemy, with desperate courage and increased strength, attempted to assail the redoubt, and would have carried it, but for the timely aid of two Continental battalions despatched by Sullivan to support his almost exhausted troops. It was in repelling these furious onsets, that the newly raised black regiment, under Col. Greene, distinguished itself by deeds of desperate valor. Posted behind a thicket in the valley, they three times drove back the Hessians, who charged repeatedly down the hill to dislodge them ; and so determined were the enemy in these successive charges, that, the day after the battle, the Hessian colonel, upon whom this duty had devolved, applied to exchange his command, and go to New York, because he dared not lead his regiment again to battle, lest his men should shoot him for having caused them so much loss." — *Arnold's History of Rhode Island*, vol. ii. pp. 427, 428.

Colonel Greene's Black Regiment.

Three years later, these soldiers are thus mentioned by the Marquis de Chastellux : —

Negro soldiers in Rhode Island.

"The 5th [of January, 1781] I did not set out till eleven, although I had thirty miles' journey to Lebanon. At the passage to the ferry, I met with a detachment of the Rhode-Island regiment, — the same corps we had with us all the last summer; but they have since been recruited and clothed. The greatest part of them are negroes or mulattoes: but they are strong, robust men; and those I have seen had a very good appearance." — *Chastellux' Travels*, vol. i. p. 454; London, 1789.

When Colonel Greene was surprised and murdered, near Points Bridge, New York, on the 14th of May, 1781, his colored soldiers heroically defended him till they were cut to pieces, and the enemy reached him over the dead bodies of his faithful negroes.

Negro soldiers in Massachusetts.

In the spring of 1778, the General Court of Massachusetts, also, was invoked to sanction the enlisting of negro soldiers. This would not have been without a precedent in her earlier legislation; for, in 1652, "negroes, Indians, and Scotchmen" (the indented captives of Cromwell, who had encountered his army at the battle of Dunbar), were alike, by law, obliged to train in the militia. In 1656, the law was altered so as to exempt "negroes and Indians"; but again, in 1660, a new law required "*every person* above the age of sixteen years" to train, except certain classes of persons specified, and "except one servant of every magistrate and teaching elder, and the sons and servants of the Major-General for the time being." Those who are curious in tracing the early legislation on the subject will notice the continuance of this vacillation into the next century.

On the 3d and the 7th of April, 1778, just before the doings of the Rhode-Island General Assembly were communicated to the Legislature of Massachusetts, Thomas Kench, belonging to a regiment of artillery then at Castle Island, addressed to the General Court the following letters, which speak for themselves: —

" *To the Honorable Council, and House of Representatives, Boston, or*
at Roxbury.

" HONORED GENTLEMEN, — At the opening of this campaign, our
forces should be all ready, well equipped with arms and ammunition,
with clothing sufficient to stand them through the campaign, their
wages to be paid monthly, so as not to give the soldiery so much
reason of complaint as it is the general cry from the soldiery amongst
whom I am connected.

" We have accounts of large re-enforcements a-coming over this
spring against us ; and we are not so strong this spring, I think, as
we were last. Great numbers have deserted ; numbers have died,
besides what is sick, and incapable of duty, or bearing arms in the
field.

" I think it is highly necessary that some new augmentation should
be added to the army this summer, — all the re-enforcements that can
possibly be obtained. For now is the time to exert ourselves or
never ; for, if the enemy can get no further hold this campaign than
they now possess, we [have] no need to fear much from them hereafter.

" A re-enforcement can quick be raised of two or three hundred
men. Will your honors grant the liberty, and give me the command
of the party ? And what I refer to is negroes. We have divers of
them in our service, mixed with white men. But I think it would be
more proper to raise a body by themselves, than to have them intermixed with the white men ; and their ambition would entirely be to out-
do the white men in every measure that the fortune of war calls a soldier
to endure. And I could rely with dependence upon them in the field
of battle, or to any post that I was sent to defend with them ; and
they would think themselves happy could they gain their freedom by
bearing a part of subduing the enemy that is invading our land, and
clear a peaceful inheritance for their masters, and posterity yet to
come, that they are now slaves to.

" The method that I would point out to your Honors in raising a
detachment of negroes ; — that a company should consist of a hundred,
including commissioned officers ; and that the commissioned officers
should be white, and consist of one captain, one captain-lieutenant,
two second lieutenants ; the orderly sergeant white ; and that there
should be three sergeants black, four corporals black, two drums and
two fifes black, and eighty-four rank and file. These should engage

to serve till the end of the war, and then be free men. And I doubt
not, that no gentleman that is a friend to his country will disapprove
of this plan, or be against his negroes enlisting into the service to
maintain the cause of freedom, and suppress the worse than savage
enemies of our land.

"I beg your Honors to grant me the liberty of raising one company, if no more. It will be far better than to fill up our battalions
with runaways and deserters from Gen. Burgoyne's army, who, after
receiving clothing and the bounty, in general make it their business to
desert from us. In the lieu thereof, if they are [of] a mind to serve
in America, let them supply the families of those gentlemen where
those negroes belong that should engage.

"I rest, relying on your Honors' wisdom in this matter, as it will
be a quick way of having a re-enforcement to join the grand army, or
to act in any other place that occasion shall require; and I will give
my faith and assurance that I will act upon honor and fidelity, should
I take the command of such a party as I have been describing.

"So I rest till your Honors shall call me; and am your very humble and obedient servant,

"THOMAS KENCH,
"In Col. Craft's Regiment of Artillery, now on Castle Island.
"CASTLE ISLAND, April 3, 1778."

" *To the Honorable Council in Boston.*

"The letter I wrote before I heard of the disturbance with Col.
Scares, Mr. Spear, and a number of other gentlemen, concerning the
freedom of negroes, in Congress Street. It is a pity that riots should
be committed on the occasion, as it is justifiable that negroes should
have their freedom, and none amongst us be held as slaves, as freedom
and liberty is the grand controversy that we are contending for; and
I trust, under the smiles of Divine Providence, we shall obtain it, if
all our minds can but be united; and putting the negroes into the
service will prevent much uneasiness, and give more satisfaction to
those that are offended at the thoughts of their servants being free.

"I will not enlarge, for fear I should give offence; but subscribe
myself   Your faithful servant,

"THOMAS KENCH.
"CASTLE ISLAND, April 7, 1778."

(MS. Archives of Massachusetts, vol. cxcix. pp. 80, 84.)

On the 11th of April, the former of the above letters was *Negro soldiers in Massachusetts.* duly referred to a joint committee, "to consider the same, and report." On the 17th, "a resolution of the General Assembly of Rhode Island for enlisting negroes in the public service" was referred to the same committee. On the 28th, they reported the draught of a law, differing little from the Rhode-Island Resolution: but a separate organization of negro companies, by Kench, does not appear to have been deemed advisable at that time; and the usage was continued, of "having," in the words of Kench, "negroes in our service, intermixed with the white men."

Many other specimens of legislative action on the subject in the Northern and Middle States might be produced; but enough have already been given to show the general current of public sentiment in this part of the country. An extract from a letter to Washington, written by John Cadwalader at Annapolis, Md., June 5, 1781, relates to the doings of that State: —

"We have resolved to raise, immediately, seven hundred and fifty *Negro soldiers in Maryland.* negroes, to be incorporated with the other troops; and a bill is now almost completed." — *Sparks's Correspondence of the American Revolution*, vol. iii. p. 331.

In an act passed by the Legislature of New York, March 20, 1781, for the purpose of raising two regiments upon the inducement of "bounty lands unappropriated," is to be found the following section: —

"Sect. 6. — And be it further enacted by the authority aforesaid, *Negro soldiers in New York.* that any person who shall deliver one or more of his or her able-bodied male slaves to any warrant officer, as aforesaid, to serve in either of the said regiments or independent corps, and produce a certificate thereof, signed by any person authorized to muster and receive the men to be raised by virtue of this act, and produce such certificate to the Surveyor-General, shall, for every male slave so entered and mustered as aforesaid, be entitled to the location and grant of one right, in manner as in and by this act is directed; and shall be, and

Negro soldiers in New York. hereby is, discharged from any future maintenance of such slave, any law to the contrary notwithstanding: And such slave so entered as aforesaid, who shall serve for the term of three years or until regularly discharged, shall, immediately after such service or discharge, be, and is hereby declared to be, a free man of this State." — *Laws of the State of New York, Chap.* 32, (*March* 20, 1781, *Fourth Session.*)

Tacitly or by positive law, the policy of arming the negroes and employing them as soldiers, either in separate companies or mingled in the ranks with white citizens, almost everywhere prevailed. In Georgia and South Carolina, however, where there was the most urgent call for more troops, and where the slave-holders were backward in enlisting, the case was different. These States, it will be remembered, contained so many Tories, whose sympathies were with the enemy, that it was impossible to obtain from them enough soldiers for a "home-guard."

It may not be amiss for Massachusetts men to refresh their memories by referring to the history of their Commonwealth in regard to supplying soldiers during the Revolution; and it may be well for all to notice, that, where there was the greatest opposition to the arming and employing of negroes as soldiers, there was the least disposition to furnish a fair supply of white soldiers. The following items of Revolutionary history were published several years since by our associate, the Hon. Lorenzo Sabine, in the historical essay prefixed to his excellent history of the "American Loyalists": —

Where the soldiers in the Continental service came from. "The whole number of regulars enlisted for the Continental service, from the beginning to the close of the struggle, was 231,959. Of these, I have once remarked, 67,907 were from Massachusetts; and I may now add, that every State south of Pennsylvania provided but 59,493, or 8,414 *less* than this single State; and that New England — now, I grieve to say, contemned and reproached — equipped and maintained 118,350, or above half of the number placed at the service of Congress during the war. I would not press these facts to the injury of the Whigs of the South. The war, after the evacuation of Boston, I am aware, was transferred from New England to the

Middle and Southern States; and these States accordingly required Where the soldiers in the Continental service came from. bodies of troops to be kept at home to protect themselves. But as it is to be presumed that most of *such bodies* composed a part of the regular force employed by Congress, and were, therefore, *included* in the Continental establishment and pay, the argument is in no essential particular weakened by the admission, that the Whigs of the South were, of necessity, employed in the defence of their own firesides; for, were this the truth of the case, *the numbers* in this service, as well as in other, would still appear, in making up the aggregate force *enlisted* from time to time in each State. The exact question is, then, not *where* were the battle-grounds of the Revolution, but what was the *proportion* of men which each of the thirteen States *supplied* for the contest.

"In considering the political condition of Virginia and North Carolina, it was admitted that these States were not able to provide troops according to their population, as compared with the States destitute of a 'peculiar institution.' The same admission is now made in behalf of South Carolina. Yet did 6,660 Whig soldiers exhaust her resources of men? Could she furnish only 752 *more* than Rhode Island, the smallest State in the Confederacy; only one-fifth of the number of Connecticut; only one-half as many as New Hampshire, then almost an unbroken wilderness? She did not: she could not defend herself against her own Tories; and it is hardly an exaggeration to add, that *more Whigs of other States were sent to her aid, and now lie buried in her soil, than she herself sent to every scene of strife outside of her own borders from Lexington to Yorktown.*

"South Carolina, with a Northern army to assist her, could not or would not even preserve her own capital. When news reached Connecticut that Gage had sent a force into the country, and that blood had been shed, Putnam was at work in his field. Leaving his plough in the furrow, he started for Cambridge, without changing his garments. When Stark heard the same tidings, he was sawing pine-logs, and without a coat: shutting down the gate of his mill, he commenced his journey to Boston in his shirt-sleeves. The same spirit animated the Whigs far and near; and the capital of New England was invested with fifteen thousand armed men.

"How was it at Charleston? That city was the great mart of the South, and, what Boston still is, the centre of the export and import trade of a large population. In grandeur, in splendor of buildings, in decorations, in equipages, in shipping and commerce, Charleston was

17

equal to any city in America. But its citizens did not rally to save it; and Gen. Lincoln was compelled to accept of terms of capitulation. He was much censured for the act. Yet whoever calmly examines the circumstances will be satisfied, I think, that the measure was unavoidable; and that the inhabitants, as a body, preferred to return to their allegiance to the British Crown. The people, on whom Congress and Gen. Lincoln depended to complete his force, refused to enlist under the Whig banner; but, after the surrender of the city, they flocked to the royal standard by hundreds. In a word, so general was the defection, that persons who had enjoyed Lincoln's confidence joined the royal side; and men who had participated in his councils bowed their necks anew to the yoke of Colonial vassalage. Sir Henry Clinton considered his triumph complete, and communicated to the ministry the intelligence that the whole State had yielded submission to the royal arms, and had become again a part of the empire. To the women of South Carolina, and to Marion, Sumpter, and Pickens, the celebrated partisan chiefs, who kept the field without the promise of men, money, or supplies, it was owing that Sir Henry's declaration did not prove entirely true for a time, and that the name and the spirit of liberty did not become utterly extinct." — *The American Loyalists*, pp. 30–33, (as corrected by the author for a second edition.)

This statement was not allowed to pass without contradiction, and the author of it was fiercely reproached. His facts and figures were called in question; but they were not proved to be incorrect. From a recent careful examination of the statistics as contained in the official report of General Knox, the Secretary of War, made to Congress in 1790, I am satisfied that Mr. Sabine, in this case, has not departed from his general practice of stating with scrupulous accuracy and impartiality the simple facts relating to his subject.

The difficulty of obtaining a sufficient number of white soldiers in the Southern States to defend them from the invasion of the enemy, and the fact that the employment of negroes, where the practice had prevailed, had proved entirely successful, led to a vigorous effort in Congress and elsewhere to take advantage of this class of persons for increasing the army, particularly in Georgia and South Carolina. Colonel John Laurens, of South Carolina, was one of the most earnest advocates of the measure. His father, the Hon. Henry Laurens, on the 16th of March, 1779, wrote to Washington:—

" Our affairs in the Southern department are more favorable than we had considered them a few days ago ; nevertheless, the country is greatly distressed, and will be more so unless further reinforcements are sent to its relief. Had we arms for three thousand such black men as I could select in Carolina, I should have no doubt of success in driving the British out of Georgia, and subduing East Florida, before the end of July." — *Sparks's Washington*, vol. vi. p. 204, note.

> Henry Laurens to Washington.

In his reply to Mr. Laurens, on the 20th of the same month, Washington, with his characteristic caution and modesty, suggests his doubts, but adds that they are " only the first crude ideas " that struck him.

> Washington to Henry Laurens.

" The policy of our arming slaves, is, in my opinion, a moot point, unless the enemy set the example. For, should we begin to form battalions of them, I have not the smallest doubt, if the war is to be prosecuted, of their following us in it, and justifying the measure upon our own ground. The contest then must be, who can arm fastest. And where are our arms? Besides, I am not clear that a discrimination will not render slavery more irksome to those who remain in it. Most of the good and evil things in this life are judged of by comparison; and I fear a comparison in this case will be productive of much discontent in those who are held in servitude. But, as this is a subject that has never employed much of my thoughts, these are no more than the first crude ideas that have struck me upon the occasion." — *Sparks's Washington*, vol. vi. p. 204.

Alexander Hamilton, who had thought much on the subject, and had considered it in its various relations, gave his unqualified and hearty support to the measure. In a letter to Mr. Jay, which has been preserved and published, he states his views with great clearness:—

"To JOHN JAY.

Alexander
Hamilton.

"DEAR SIR, — Col. Laurens, who will have the honor of deliver-ing you this letter, is on his way to South Carolina, on a project which I think, in the present situation of affairs there, is a very good one, and deserves every kind of support and encouragement. This is, to raise two, three, or four battalions of negroes, with the assist-ance of the government of that State, by contributions from the owners, in proportion to the number they possess. If you should think proper to enter upon the subject with him, he will give you a detail of his plan. He wishes to have it recommended by Congress to the State; and, as an inducement, that they should engage to take those battalions into Continental pay.

"It appears to me, that an expedient of this kind, in the present state of Southern affairs, is the most rational that can be adopted, and promises very important advantages. Indeed, I hardly see how a sufficient force can be collected in that quarter without it; and the enemy's operations there are growing infinitely more serious and formidable. I have not the least doubt that the negroes will make very excellent soldiers with proper management; and I will venture to pronounce, that they cannot be put into better hands than those of Mr. Laurens. He has all the zeal, intelligence, enterprise, and every other qualification, necessary to succeed in such an undertaking. It is a maxim with some great military judges, that, with sensible offi-cers, soldiers can hardly be too stupid; and, on this principle, it is thought that the Russians would make the best troops in the world, if they were under other officers than their own. The King of Prussia is among the number who maintain this doctrine; and has a very emphatic saying on the occasion, which I do not exactly recollect. I mention this because I hear it frequently objected to the scheme of embodying negroes, that they are too stupid to make soldiers. This is so far from appearing to me a valid objection, that I think their want of cultivation (for their natural faculties are probably as good as ours), joined to that habit of subordination which they acquire from a life of servitude, will make them sooner become soldiers than our white inhabitants. Let officers be men of sense and sentiment; and the nearer the soldiers approach to machines, perhaps the better.

"I foresee that this project will have to combat much opposition from prejudice and self-interest. The contempt we have been taught to entertain for the blacks makes us fancy many things that are foundod neither in reason nor experience; and an unwillingness to part with property of so valuable a kind will furnish a thousand arguments to show the impracticability or pernicious tendency of a scheme which requires such a sacrifice. But it should be considered, that, if we do not make use of them in this way, the enemy probably will; and that the best way to counteract the temptations they will hold out will be to offer them ourselves. An essential part of the plan is to give them their freedom with their muskets. This will secure their fidelity, animate their courage, and, I believe, will have a good influence upon those who remain, by opening a door to their emancipation. This circumstance, I confess, has no small weight in inducing me to wish the success of the project; for the dictates of humanity, and true policy, equally interest me in favor of this unfortunate class of men.

Alexander Hamilton.

 " With the truest respect and esteem,
" I am, Sir, your most obedient servant,
" ALEX. HAMILTON."
(Life of John Jay, by William Jay, vol. ii. pp. 31, 32.)

 Congress, although it had no power to control the action of the individual States in this matter, considered the subject so important, that it was referred to a special committee, who prepared a report, that led to the adoption of a series of resolutions, recommending to " the States of South Carolina and Georgia, if they shall think the same expedient, to take measures immediately for raising three thousand able-bodied negroes."

Congress recommends negro enlistments.

" IN CONGRESS, March 29, 1779.
 " The Committee, consisting of Mr. Burke, Mr. Laurens, Mr. Armstrong, Mr. Wilson, and Mr. Dyer, appointed to take into consideration the circumstances of the Southern States, and the ways and means for their safety and defence, report, —

  . . . . .

 " That the State of South Carolina, as represented by the delegates of the said State and by Mr. Huger, who has come hither, at the request of the Governor of the said State, on purpose to explain the particular circumstances thereof, is unable to make any effectual efforts with militia, by reason of the great proportion of citizens necessary to remain at home to prevent insurrections among the negroes, and to prevent the desertion of them to the enemy.

"That the state of the country, and the great numbers of those people among them, expose the inhabitants to great danger from the endeavors of the enemy to excite them either to revolt or desert.

"That it is suggested by the delegates of the said State and by Mr. Huger, that a force might be raised in the said State from among the negroes, which would not only be formidable to the enemy from their numbers, and the discipline of which they would very readily admit, but would also lessen the danger from revolts and desertions, by detaching the most vigorous and enterprising from among the negroes.

"That, as this measure may involve inconveniences peculiarly affecting the States of South Carolina and Georgia, the Committee are of opinion that the same should be submitted to the governing powers of the said States; and, if the said powers shall judge it expedient to raise such a force, that the United States ought to defray the expense thereof: whereupon,

"Resolved, That it be recommended to the States of South Carolina and Georgia, if they shall think the same expedient, to take measures immediately for raising three thousand able-bodied negroes.

"That the said negroes be formed into separate corps, as battalions, according to the arrangements adopted for the main army, to be commanded by white commissioned and non-commissioned officers.

"That the commissioned officers be appointed by the said States.

"That the non-commissioned officers may, if the said States respectively shall think proper, be taken from among the non-commissioned officers and soldiers of the Continental battalions of the said States respectively.

"That the Governors of the said States, together with the commanding officer of the Southern army, be empowered to incorporate the several Continental battalions of their States with each other respectively, agreeably to the arrangement of the army, as established by the resolutions of May 27, 1778; and to appoint such of the supernumerary officers to command the said negroes as shall choose to go into that service.

"Resolved, That Congress will make provision for paying the proprietors of such negroes as shall be enlisted for the service of the United States during the war a full compensation for the property, at a rate not exceeding one thousand dollars for each active, able-

bodied negro man of standard size, not exceeding thirty-five years of Congress recommends negro enlistments.
age, who shall be so enlisted and pass muster.

"That no pay or bounty be allowed to the said negroes; but that
they be clothed and subsisted at the expense of the United States.

"That every negro who shall well and faithfully serve as a soldier
to the end of the present war, and shall then return his arms, be
emancipated, and receive the sum of fifty dollars." — *Secret Journals
of Congress*, vol. i. pp. 107–110.

On the same day that the report in favor of raising negro
troops was made, Congress passed the following resolution: —

"Whereas John Laurens, Esq., who has heretofore acted as
aide-de-camp to the Commander-in-chief, is desirous of repairing to
South Carolina, with a design to assist in defence of the Southern
States; —

"*Resolved*, That a commission of lieutenant-colonel be granted to
the said John Laurens, Esq." — *Journals of Congress*, vol. v. p. 123.

Col. John Laurens was the son of the Hon. Henry Laurens,
the distinguished member of Congress and at one time
President of that body. He was one of the most patriotic
and brave of the Southern officers, and has not improperly
been called the "Chevalier Bayard of America." He was
the intimate friend of Washington and Hamilton. Having
been in active service in Rhode Island and elsewhere, and
having had the best opportunities of witnessing the usefulness of the colored soldiers, he entered into the spirit of the
undertaking with his whole heart, and used his best efforts to
promote its success. For this purpose, he went to his native
State, and used his personal influence to induce the Legislature to take the necessary steps for raising black troops. In
a letter to Hamilton, he says, —

"Ternant will relate to you how many violent struggles I have Colonel Laurens.
had between duty and inclination, — how much my heart was with
you, while I appeared to be most actively employed here. But it
appears to me, that I should be inexcusable in the light of a citizen,
if I did not continue my utmost efforts for carrying the plan of the

black levies into execution, while there remain the smallest hopes of success." — *Works of Hamilton*, vol. i. pp. 114, 115.

On the 14th of February, 1780, Col. Laurens wrote to Washington from Charleston: —

Colonel Laurens.

" Private accounts say that General Prevost is left to command at Savannah ; that his troops consist of the Hessians and Loyalists that were there before, re-enforced by a corps of blacks and a detachment of savages. It is generally reported that Sir Henry Clinton commands the present expedition." — *Sparks's Correspondence of the American Revolution*, vol. ii. p. 402.

Sir Henry Clinton's Proclamation.

It should be borne in mind that Sir Henry Clinton had several months previously issued a proclamation, calling upon negroes to join his army, either as soldiers, or with full security to follow any occupation within his lines which they thought proper. This proclamation was first printed in New York, in Rivington's " Royal Gazette," on the 3d of July, 1779. It is here reprinted from that journal. The words in Italics were added in the issue of August 25th, with a note stating that they had, " through the mistake of the printers, been hitherto omitted."

" By his Excellency Sir HENRY CLINTON, K.B. General and Commander-in-chief of all his Majesty's Forces within the Colonies laying on the Atlantic Ocean, from Nova Scotia to West-Florida, inclusive, &c., &c., &c.

PROCLAMATION.

" Whereas the enemy have adopted a practice of enrolling NEGROES among their Troops, I do hereby give notice That all NEGROES taken in arms, or upon any military Duty, shall be purchased for *the public service at* a stated Price ; the money to be paid to the Captors.

" But I do most strictly forbid any Person to sell or claim Right over any NEGROE, the property of a Rebel, who may take Refuge with any part of this Army: And I do promise to every NEGROE who shall desert the Rebel Standard, full security to follow within these Lines, any Occupation which he shall think proper.

" Given under my Hand, at Head-Quarters, PHILIPSBURGH, the 30th day of June, 1779.   " H. CLINTON.

" By his Excellency's command,
⸳   "JOHN SMITH, Secretary."

Lord Cornwallis also issued a proclamation encouraging the slaves to join the British Army; but it is well known that no regard for their welfare prompted his action, and but little kindness was shown by him to the slaves who deserted their masters, or who were compelled to leave them. A letter from Mr. Jefferson to Dr. Gordon, written several years after the war was closed, contains a passage which shows how that statesman regarded the treatment of his own negroes. *Lord Cornwallis's Proclamation.*

"Lord Cornwallis destroyed all my growing crops of corn and tobacco; he burned all my barns, containing the same articles of the last year, having first taken what corn he wanted; he used, as was to be expected, all my stock of cattle, sheep, and hogs, for the sustenance of his army, and carried off all the horses capable of service; of those too young for service he cut the throats; and he burned all the fences on the plantation, so as to leave it an absolute waste. *He carried off also about thirty slaves. Had this been to give them freedom, he would have done right;* but it was to consign them to inevitable death from the small-pox and putrid fever, then raging in his camp. This I knew afterwards to be the fate of twenty-seven of them. I never had news of the remaining three, but presume they shared the same fate. When I say that Lord Cornwallis did all this, I do not mean that he carried about the torch in his own hands, but that it was all done under his eye; the situation of the house, in which he was, commanding a view of every part of the plantation, so that he must have seen every fire. I relate these things on my own knowledge, in a great degree, as I was on the ground soon after he left it. He treated the rest of the neighborhood somewhat in the same style, but not with that spirit of total extermination with which he seemed to rage over my possessions. Wherever he went, the dwelling-houses were plundered of every thing which could be carried off. Lord Cornwallis's character in England would forbid the belief that he shared in the plunder; but that his table was served with the plate thus pillaged from private houses, can be proved by many hundred eye-witnesses. From an estimate I made at that time, on the best information I could collect, I supposed *the State of Virginia lost, under Lord Cornwallis's hand, that year, about thirty thousand slaves; and that, of these, twenty-seven thousand died of the* *Thomas Jefferson to Doctor Gordon.*

small-pox and camp-fever; and the rest were partly sent to the West Indies, and exchanged for rum, sugar, coffee, and fruit; and partly sent to New York, from whence they went, at the peace, either to Nova Scotia or to England. From this last place, I believe, they have been lately sent to Africa. History will never relate the horrors committed by the British Army in the Southern States of America." — *Jefferson's Works*, vol. ii. p. 426.

It is very evident from this statement, that the distrust and fears on the part of the negroes, in regard to the promises of the British officers, Dunmore, Clinton, and Cornwallis, were well founded. In striking contrast to their treatment of the slaves is the noble sentiment of Jefferson, himself a severe sufferer from the conduct of Cornwallis: "*Had this been to give them freedom, he would have done right.*"

In the autumn of the year 1780, Colonel Laurens was sent on an important mission to France. The policy which he so warmly advocated in his own State and in Georgia was not, however, neglected during his absence.

General Lincoln repeatedly and earnestly implored that the army in the South might be strengthened in this, which seemed to be the only practicable way. In a letter to Governor Rutledge, dated Charleston, March 13, 1780, he says : —

General Lincoln.

"Give me leave to add once more, that I think the measure of raising a black corps a necessary one ; that I have great reason to believe, if permission is given for it, that many men would soon be obtained. I have repeatedly urged this matter, not only because Congress have recommended it, and because it thereby becomes my duty to attempt to have it executed, but because my own mind suggests the utility and importance of the measure, as the safety of the town makes it necessary." — *Manuscript Letter.*

Mr. Madison, in a letter to Joseph Jones, dated November 20, 1780, thus advocated the policy of freeing and arming the negroes : —

James Madison.

"Yours of the 18th came yesterday. I am glad to find the Legislature persist in their resolution to recruit their line of the army for the war; though, without deciding on the expediency of the mode under their consideration, would it not be as well to liberate and make soldiers at once of the blacks themselves, as to make them instruments for enlisting white soldiers? It would certainly be more consonant with the principles of liberty, which ought never to be lost sight of in a contest for liberty: and, with white officers and a majority of white soldiers, no imaginable danger could be feared from themselves, as there certainly could be none from the effect of the example on those who should remain in bondage; experience having shown that a freedman immediately loses all attachment and sympathy with his former fellow-slaves." — *Madison Papers*, p. 68. *James Madison.*

On the 28th of February, 1781, General Greene, who was then in North Carolina, wrote to Washington: —

"The enemy have ordered two regiments of negroes to be immediately embodied, and are drafting a great proportion of the young men of that State [South Carolina], to serve during the war." — *Sparks's Correspondence of the American Revolution*, vol. iii. p. 246. *General Greene.*

Colonel Laurens, some time after his return from France, resumed his efforts to induce the slaveholders of South Carolina and Georgia to allow their negroes to enlist as soldiers in the Continental Army; and, although he found that "truth and philosophy had gained some ground," he was compelled to say that "the single voice of reason was drowned by the howlings of a triple-headed monster, in which prejudice, avarice, and pusillanimity were united." Two letters, written by him only a few months before he laid down his life for his country in battle, contain further evidence of his faithful efforts, and a sad account of the manner in which his purposes were defeated. Both of these letters were addressed to Washington. The first was dated May 19, 1782.

"The plan which brought me to this country was urged with all the zeal which the subject inspired, both in our Privy Council and Assembly; but the single voice of reason was drowned by the howlings of a triple-headed monster, in which prejudice, avarice, and pusillanimity were united. It was some degree of consolation to me, however, to perceive that truth and philosophy had gained some *Colonel Laurens to Washington.*

ground; the suffrages in favor of the measure being twice as numerous as on a former occasion.   Some hopes have been lately given
me from Georgia; but I fear, when the question is put, we shall be
outvoted there with as much disparity as we have been in this
country.

     .   .   .   .   .

"I earnestly desire to be where any active plans are likely to be
executed, and to be near your Excellency on all occasions in which
my services can be acceptable.   The pursuit of an object which, I
confess, is a favorite one with me, because I always regarded the
interests of this country and those of the Union as intimately connected with it, has detached me more than once from your family;
but those sentiments of veneration and attachment with which your
Excellency has inspired me, keep me always near you, with the sin-
cerest and most zealous wishes for a continuance of your happiness
and glory." — *Sparks's Correspondence of the American Revolution,*
vol. iii. p. 506.

The last letter was dated June 12, 1782; and from it we
learn that his hope of accomplishing something in this way
clung to him to the last.

"The approaching session of the Georgia Legislature, and the
encouragement given me by Governor Howley, who has a decisive
influence in the counsels of that country, induce me to remain in this
quarter for the purpose of taking new measures on the subject of our
black levies.   The arrival of Colonel Baylor, whose seniority entitles
him to the command of the light troops, affords me ample leisure for
pursuing the business in person; and I shall do it with all the tenacity
of a man making a last effort on so interesting an occasion." — .
Sparks's Correspondence of the American Revolution, vol. iii. p. 515.

Washington, however, seems to have lost all faith in the
patriotism of the men who continued to refuse aid to their
suffering country in the only practicable way which had been
suggested.   He has seldom said any thing so severe as the
following words, in his reply to the first of the above letters: —

"I must confess that I am not at all astonished at the failure of
your plan.   That spirit of freedom, which, at the commencement

of this contest, would have gladly sacrificed every thing to the attain- ^{Washing-} ment of its object, has long since subsided, and every selfish passion has taken its place. It is not the public but private interest which influences the generality of mankind; nor can the Americans any longer boast an exception. Under these circumstances, it would rather have been suprising if you had succeeded; nor will you, I fear, have better success in Georgia." — *Sparks's Washington*, vol. iii. pp. 322, 323.

Washing-
ton to Colo-
nel Lau-
rens.

The friend and associate of Colonel Laurens, as a member of Washington's family, and a fellow-soldier in more than one battle, Colonel David Humphreys, gave the sanction of his name and the influence of his popularity to the raising of colored troops in Connecticut.

Colonel
Hum-
phreys.

"In November, 1782, he was, by resolution of Congress, commissioned as a Lieutenant-Colonel, with order that his commission should bear date from the 23d of June, 1780, when he received his appointment as aid-de-camp to the Commander-in-chief. He had, when in active service, given the sanction of his name and influence in the establishment of a company of colored infantry, attached to Meigs', afterwards Butler's, regiment, in the Connecticut line. He continued to be the nominal captain of that company until the establishment of peace." — *Biographical Sketch in "The National Portrait Gallery of Distinguished Americans."*

Lord Dunmore's efforts to secure the services of negroes, at the commencement of the Revolutionary War, are well known; his proclamation, and the action of the Virginia Convention upon it, having been published at the time, and the matter having occasioned much comment since. By the courtesy of Mr. Bancroft, who has kindly put into my hands the *unpublished original manuscript* of the following letter and "sketch," and also a copy of Lord Dunmore's private letter to Sir Henry Clinton enclosing them, I am now enabled to present the views of his Lordship on the subject seven years later, and just before the close of hostilities.

Lord Dun-
more.

TO THE RIGHT HONORABLE EARL DUNMORE, &C.

"CHARLES TOWN, 5th January, 1782.

Proposal to Lord Dunmore.

"MY LORD,—Since I had the honor of seeing your Lordship, I have revolved in my mind the subject-matter of our conversation; and the more I think, the more I am convinced of the magnitude and national importance of the object. It is long since I beheld the scheme in the most favorable point of view, and often have I strenuously recommended it. There were, at the time the thought first seriously made an impression on my mind, some very powerful and uncontrovertible reasons; namely, the impossibility, that I foresaw, of maintaining and supporting troops from Europe, in the low parts of this country, during the sickly season. The fall months have caused such mortality in 1780 at the outposts, that no country on earth, at such a distance, could support the loss of men. Another reason that operated on my mind, added to the eagerness I observed in the generality of the people under my direction to have arms put into their hands on the incursions of the enemy, even while we had troops at Camden, preventing the negroes from being of any service to Government in planting and cultivating the land; what, with the proofs they have given, on various occasions, of spirit and enterprise, left me no room to doubt that they might be employed to the utmost advantage. While there was a ray of hope left for believing that Lord Cornwallis had made his escape with a small part of his army, I was easy and happy, convinced that he would not have hesitated a moment in giving freedom to men of all complexions that would faithfully serve the King, and assist in crushing a most infernal rebellion. And I cannot help thinking, my Lord, that there is something peculiarly fortunate in your Lordship's arrival here at this very critical moment; for next to Lord Cornwallis, who has the advantage of military rank in the empire, there is none so able to form and execute so great a design, nor in whom the King's friends have equal confidence as in your Lordship. Unless some vigorous step is taken, I humbly think it is more than probable that the nation at large will insist on this American War being relinquished. What can Administration say, what can they promise themselves or the nation, by a prosecution of the war in such hands? Nothing but ultimate ruin.

"If, my Lord, this scheme is adopted, arranged, and ready for being put in execution, the moment the troops penetrate into the country after the arrival of the promised re-enforcements, America is to be conquered with its own force (I mean the Provincial troops and the black troops to be raised), and the British and Hessian army could be spared to attack the French where they are most vulnerable. The nation would, by that means, be relieved from an amazing burthen, — that of supporting the army at New York, — what has been a sink of treasure, and a bed of voluptuousness and dissipation. I say, my Lord, if the British and Hessian troops were ordered to leave the country, only sending force sufficient to garrison Rhode Island, that your Lordship and my friend Gov. Martin, with the Provincial troops, the King's friends, and the new levies, would soon possess the three Southern provinces, in spite of all the force the rebels could assemble. 'T is notorious that more than two-thirds of North Carolina have expressed an eager desire for the re-establishment of British government. They have given striking proofs of zeal, spirit, and enterprise; and under the direction of those they love, and who would reward their merit, rebellion would soon cease to exist on the south side of James River. Pardon me, my Lord, for this tedious digression. Such a variety of new matter crowds upon me, that I could not help giving my thoughts a place.

"It may, and I dare say will, be said by Opposition, 'What! arm the slaves? We shudder at the very idea, so repugnant to humanity, so barbarous and shocking to human nature,' &c. One very simple answer is, in my mind, to be given: Whether is it better to make this vast continent become an acquisition of power, strength, and consequence to Great Britain again, or tamely give it up to France, who will reap the fruits of American Independence, to the utter ruin of Britain? It may be said, 'How can you do such an injury to your friends?' In the first place, our friends in this province are not numerous whose property consists in slaves. The friends of Britain in the Southern provinces, in general, are the merchants; and they have little property in slaves. And, in the second place, I deny that we injure our friends by giving freedom to those slaves that are proper for soldiers. 'T is only changing one master for another; and let it be clearly understood that they are to serve the King for ever, and that those slaves who are not taken for his Majesty's service are to remain on the plantation, and perform, as usual, the labor of the field; and, so far from ruining the property, I do aver, and experience will, I doubt not, justify the assertion, that, by embodying the most hardy, intrepid, and determined blacks, they would not only keep the rest in good order, but, by being disciplined and under command, be prevented from rais-

Proposal to Lord Dunmore.

Proposal to Lord Dunmore.

ing cabals, tumults, and even rebellion, what I think might be expected soon after a peace; but so far from making even our lukewarm friends and secret foes greater enemies by this measure, I will, by taking their slaves, engage to make them better friends. This, my Lord, may appear enigmatical; but your Lordship's experience of mankind in general, and of the people in this country in particular, will do justice to my opinion, that if the nation had, instead of lavishing her treasure, and opening a very wide door for her servants to heap up wealth at her expense, and feeding and supporting, by her gold that circulates in the country, that very rebellion she wished to crush; I say, my Lord, that [had] she, instead of paying money for all necessaries purchased for the use of the army, granted receipts, bearing interest so long as the holders remained loyal, and a promise to pay the principal at the expiration of the rebellion, — our affairs would have been in a very different situation to-day.

"I have, my Lord, done myself the honor to enclose a sketch of a plan for embodying ten thousand men; and I would beg leave to suggest to your Lordship the propriety of laying your plan before Col. Moncrief, and offering him a brigade, with your Lordship's interest to secure him the rank of brigadier-general. I can assure you of a certainty, that it will be by much the best channel in which it can be placed; and I would humbly recommend to your Lordship to make it known only to Moncrief, who, with yourself, is fully equal to set it on its legs. I am afraid, my Lord, that I have wearied your patience. My motives I beg you may believe to be most pure; and I have the honor to be, my Lord, your Lordship's most obedient and most humble servant,   "J. CRUDEN."

"CHARLES TOWN, 5th January, 1782.

Sketch of a plan for arming the negroes.

"In the Province of South Carolina, ten thousand Black Troops may be raised, inured to fatigue and to the climate, without impoverishing the plantations so much that they might not be able to produce crops equal to the maintenance and support, not only of the women and children that are left on the estates, but also sufficient to feed, clothe, and pay the Black Troops.

"When these men are raised, there can be no doubt, that, with the force here, they will be able to drive the enemy from the Province, and open a large door for our friends from North Carolina to join us, till such time as it may be policy, and we may have a sufficient command of the sea, to enter Virginia.

"When the country is again in our possession, with proper and Sketch of a plan for arming the negroes. effectual support, I will engage to maintain and clothe those Black Troops from the estates of the enemy; and I will also engage to pay the interest of the receipts granted to our friends, at the rate of eight per cent. And, to convince the world that we never adopt any measure at the expense of individuals, let three or more gentlemen of the country — men of honor and probity — be appointed to value the negroes that belong to our friends, and at the rate they would have sold for in 1773, and Government to be accountable for the amount at the expiration of the war, paying interest at the customary rate, so long as the parties concerned maintained their allegiance.

"That, for all negroes, the property of the enemy, the adjutant-general to grant receipts to the commissioner of sequestered estates, and returns made to him when they are killed, or lost to the service, that others may be furnished to supply their place.

"It is impossible to conceive or think what the effects of such a measure would be. Striking at the root of all property, and making the wealth and riches of the enemy the means of bringing them to obedience, must bring the most violent to their senses. Such a wonderful change may it work, that I would not be surprised, that those now most violent against us would be foremost in an application for peace on our own terms.

"Property, all the world over, is dear to mankind; and in this country they are as much wedded to it as in any other; and, in the Southern Provinces, men are great in proportion to the number of their slaves.

"I should think that one major-general, two brigadier-generals, six lieutenant-colonels commandant, twelve majors and twelve adjutants, ninety-six captains, one hundred and ninety-two lieutenants, with quartermasters, &c., &c., &c., would be equal to discipline and command ten thousand men.

"J. CRUDEN."

EARL OF DUNMORE TO SIR HENRY CLINTON.

"CHARLES TOWN, Feb. 2, 1782.

"SIR, — I was in hopes of having the pleasure of delivering the Lord Dunmore to Sir Henry Clinton. enclosed letters in person, but the fleet in which I came out not proceeding to New York, being advised, and thinking it unsafe to hazard a further voyage to the northward, at this season of the year, with so large a fleet.

"I should have sent you these letters by the 'Rotterdam,' had I known she meant to go to New York, as I do not know but they may be of importance. By one of them, your Excellency will see that his Majesty wished I would return to this country; we then thinking that we should have found our affairs in Virginia in a very different state from what they really are; and for which, in my humble opinion, there is now no remedy left, without adopting the following plan, or something similar to it, which I humbly submit to your serious consideration.

"I arrived here the 21st of December; and, having no employment, I made it my business to converse with every one that I thought capable of giving me any good information of the real situation of this country: and every one that I have conversed with think, and, I must own, my own sentiments perfectly coincide with theirs, that the most efficacious, expeditious, cheapest, and certain means of reducing this country to a proper sense of their duty is in employing the blacks, who are, in my opinion, not only better fitted for service in this warm climate than white men, but they are also better guides, may be got on much easier terms, and are perfectly attached to our sovereign. And, by employing them, you cannot devise a means more effectual to distress your foes, not only by depriving them of their property, but by depriving them of their labor. You in reality deprive them of their existence; for, without their labor, they cannot subsist: and, from my own knowledge of them, I am sure they are as soon disciplined as any set of raw men that I know of.

"From my perfect belief of the above facts, I do most earnestly wish your Excellency would adopt the measure on some such footing as is here enclosed; and, as the strongest proof of my good opinion of the measure, I am most willing, provided you approve, and have no other person you may think better qualified to put it in execution, to hazard my reputation and person in the execution of it.

"What I would further propose is, that the officers of the Provincials, who are swarming in the streets here, perfectly idle, should be employed to command these men, with the rank they now have.

"I would also propose, at first, to raise only ten thousand Blacks, to give them white officers and non-commissioned officers, but to fill up the vacancies of the non-commissioned officers now and then with black people, as their services should entitle them to it.

"In order to induce the negroes to enlist, I would propose to give each black man one guinea and a crown, with a promise of freedom to all that should serve during the continuance of the war; and, that they may be fully satisfied that this promise will be held inviolate, it must be given by the officer appointed to command them, he being empowered so to do, in the most ample manner, by your Excellency. As there will no doubt be a great many men come in that will be unfit for military service, I would propose employing them, with the women and children, under proper managers, to cultivate any lands in our possession; and I doubt not, with proper management, to raise sufficient food for the maintenance of the black troops at least, and perhaps enough to dispose of that would both pay and clothe the whole. But should this plan fail, contrary to my most sanguine wish and real opinion, the expense will be so trifling in trying the experiment, that it can never be thought an object of the smallest consideration.

"In order to obviate the only objection that I see to this plan (namely, that of employing slaves, the property of a few friends that are with us here), I would propose that they should be valued by three gentlemen of known skill and probity, and that a receipt should be given them for the value of such slaves; paying them six per cent. interest upon it till the expiration of the war, or so long as the holders' allegiance lasted: and, if that continues to the expiration of the war, pay them the principal. And, indeed, I would propose that no money should in future be given for any thing taken from the inhabitants for the use of the troops, but receipts granted on the same terms.

" Should this plan in general meet with your Excellency's approbation, there are many more ideas relative to it that I will take another opportunity of communicating to you.

" I have wrote fully to Lord George Germain on this subject, and have sent him a copy of this letter; but I hope, before we can hear from home, you will have had the credit of adopting the plan."

(Extract.)

EARL OF DUNMORE TO SECRETARY LORD GEORGE GERMAIN.

"CHARLES TOWN, S. C., Feb. 5, 1782.

. . . . " Enclosed I send your Lordship a copy of a letter I have wrote to Sir Henry Clinton, for employing Negroes in this country."

(Extract.)

EARL OF DUNMORE TO SECRETARY LORD GEORGE GERMAIN.

"CHARLES TOWN, S. C., March 30, 1782.

" Since writing to your Lordship of the 5th of February, there has been a motion made in the Rebel Assembly of this Province for raising

Lord Dunmore to Sir Henry Clinton.

Lord Dunmore to Lord George Germain.

a brigade of negroes, which was only negatived by a very few voices, and it 's supposed will be re-assumed and carried on a future day; and we, by neglecting to make a proper use of those people, who are much attached to us, shall have them, in a short time, employed against us. They are now carrying them up the country as fast as they can find them.

"As soon as this is closed, I shall set off for New York in the ' Carysfort.' "

General Greene.

One of the ablest, most experienced, and most successful of the American generals, second only, in the estimation of many, to the Commander-in-chief,— General Nathaniel Greene, —in a letter to Washington, dated on the 24th of January, 1782, says:—

" I have recommended to this State to raise some black regiments. To fill up the regiments with whites is impracticable, and to get re-enforcements from the northwards precarious, and at least difficult, from the prejudices respecting the climate. Some are for it; but the far greater part of the people are opposed to it." — *Sparks's Correspondence of the American Revolution*, vol. iii. p. 467.

The letter of General Greene to Governor Rutledge, of South Carolina, is printed below. The opinion of such an officer, formed after the experiment of employing Negro soldiers at the North had been fully tried, and after a residence in the Southern States had enabled him to consider the subject with the advantage of an " acquaintance with the habits, character, and feelings of that class of people," is of the highest importance.

" The natural strength of the country, in point of numbers, appears to me to consist much more in the blacks than in the whites. Could they be incorporated, and employed for its defence. it would afford you double security. That they would make good soldiers, I have not the least doubt; and I am persuaded the State has it not in its power to give sufficient re-enforcements, without incorporating them, either to secure the country, if the enemy mean to act vigorously upon an offensive plan, or furnish a force sufficient to dispossess them of Charleston, should it be defensive.

"The number of whites in this State is too small, and the state of General Greene. your finances too low, to attempt to raise a force in any other way. Should the measure be adopted, it may prove a good means of preventing the enemy from further attempts upon this country, when they find they have not only the whites, but the blacks also, to contend with. And I believe it is generally agreed, that, if the natural strength of this country could have been employed in its defence, the enemy would have found it little less than impracticable to have got footing here, much more to have overrun the country, by which the inhabitants have suffered infinitely greater loss than would have been sufficient to have given you perfect security; and, I am persuaded, the incorporation of a part of the negroes would rather tend to secure the fidelity of others, than excite discontent, mutiny, and desertion among them. The force I would ask for this purpose, in addition to what we have, and what may probably join us from the Northward or from the militia of this State, would be four regiments, — two upon the Continental, and two upon the State, establishment; a corps of pioneers and a corps of artificers, each to consist of about eighty men. The two last may be either on a temporary or permanent establishment, as may be most agreeable to the State. The others should have their freedom, and be clothed and treated, in all respects, as other soldiers; without which they will be unfit for the duties expected from them."— *Johnson's Life of Greene,* vol. ii. p. 274.

The author of " Sketches of the Life and Correspondence of General Greene," himself a Southerner and a resident of Charleston, thus comments on the proposal to employ the negroes as soldiers : —

"Those who can enter into the feelings and opinions of the citizens Judge of those States which tolerate slavery will be not a little startled at the Johnson on negro proposition submitted to the Governor and Council in this letter. A soldiers. strong, deep-seated feeling, nurtured from earliest infancy, decides, with instinctive promptness, against a measure of so threatening an aspect, and so offensive to that republican pride, which disdains to commit the defence of the country to servile hands, or share with a color to which the idea of inferiority is inseparably connected the profession of arms, and that approximation of condition which must exist between the regular soldier and the militia-man.

" But the Governor and Council viewed the subject under the influence of less feeling. It seems the proposition had formerly been under consideration in the State Legislature; and, as the meeting of that board was now at hand, it was resolved to submit it to their decision.

"There is a sovereign, who, at this time, draws his soldiery from the same class of people; and finds a facility in forming and disciplining an army, which no other power enjoys. Nor does his immense military force, formed from that class of his subjects, excite the least apprehensions; for the soldier's will is subdued to that of his officer, and his improved condition takes away the habit of identifying himself with the class from which he has been separated. Military men know what mere machines men become under discipline, and believe that any men, who may be made obedient, may be made soldiers; and that increasing their numbers increases the means of their own subjection and government.

"It is now probable that the idea of forming a military force by a draught from the slaves had been suggested to Gen. Greene by a recent acquaintance with the habits, character, and feelings of that class of people. It could not escape his eye, that there was no sense of hostility existing between the master and slave, but rather something of the clannish, or patriarchal, feelings known to exist between the inhabitants of a village and their chief. He had remarked the joy expressed by the slaves on their deliverance from the tyranny of the enemy, and the return of a protector in the person of their master; and it was obvious, that if the State could give a slave for the services of a man as a soldier for ten months, as had been the case in raising some of its troops, it would be great gain to convert the same slave into a soldier for the war, to be paid only by his freedom, after having served with fidelity. But the Legislature, when it met, thought the experiment a dangerous one; and the project was relinquished. They adopted, however, the alternative of raising soldiers on the black population by giving a slave for a soldier. Parties were sent to collect slaves from the plantations of the loyalists, and rendezvous established in vain in various places in the interior country."—*Johnson's Life of Greene,* vol. ii. pp. 274, 275.

Propositions for peace were introduced in the British Parliament, and preliminary steps were taken towards the cessation of hostilities, before the letters from Lord Dunmore reached the Secretary, Lord George Germain. But these letters, and those written by Colonel Laurens and General

Greene in the last months of the Revolutionary War, are of historical importance. They contain the mature opinions and the deliberate decision of the highest British and American military authorities, in unequivocal support of the policy of arming the negro slaves, and employing them as soldiers.

The following letter, addressed to Brigadier-General Rufus Putnam, and afterwards printed, from his papers, at Marietta, Ohio, shows the tender care which the Commander-in-chief had for the rights of the negro soldiers in the army : —

"HEAD QUARTERS, Feb. 2, 1783.

"SIR, — Mr. Hobby having claimed as his property a negro man now serving in the Massachusetts Regiment, you will please to order a court of inquiry, consisting of five as respectable officers as can be found in your brigade, to examine the validity of the claim, the manner in which the person in question came into service, and the propriety of his being discharged or retained in service. Having inquired into the matter, with all the attending circumstances, they will report to you their opinion thereon; which you will report to me as soon as conveniently may be.

"I am, Sir, with great respect,

"Your most obedient servant,

"G. WASHINGTON.

"P.S. — All concerned should be notified to attend.

"Brig.-Gen. PUTNAM."

[marginal note: Washington's regard for the rights of negro soldiers.]

Luther Martin, it will be remembered, in his address to the Legislature of Maryland on the Federal Constitution, deplored the growing laxity of public sentiment on the subject of slavery. "When our liberties were at stake," he said, "we warmly felt for the common rights of men. The danger being thought to be past which threatened ourselves, we are daily growing more insensible to those rights." A sad illustration of the truth of this declaration was found in the conduct of some of the slaveholders, who, having sent their negroes to the army with the promise of personal liberty, at the close of the war attempted to re-enslave them.

To the honor of Virginia, — who could then claim Washington and Jefferson and Madison among her living patriots, — this wrong to the negro soldiers was not overlooked, nor permitted to continue. The General Assembly of that State, in 1783, enacted the following law : —

"*An Act directing the Emancipation of certain Slaves who have served as Soldiers in this State, and for the Emancipation of the Slave Aberdeen.*

Negro soldiers emancipated.

" I. Whereas it hath been represented to the present General Assembly, that, during the course of the war, many persons in this State had caused their slaves to enlist in certain regiments or corps raised within the same, having tendered such slaves to the officers appointed to recruit forces within the State, as substitutes for free persons whose lot or duty it was to serve in such regiments or corps, at the same time representing to such recruiting officers that the slaves, so enlisted by their direction and concurrence, were freemen ; and it appearing further to this Assembly, that on the expiration of the term of enlistment of such slaves, that the former owners have attempted again to force them to return to a state of servitude, contrary to the principles of justice, and to their own solemn promise ;

" II. And whereas it appears just and reasonable, that all persons enlisted as aforesaid, who have faithfully served agreeable to the terms of their enlistment, and have thereby of course contributed towards the establishment of American liberty and independence, should enjoy the blessings of freedom as a reward for their toils and labors ;

"*Be it therefore enacted*, That each and every slave who, by the appointment and direction of his owner, hath enlisted in any regiment or corps raised within this State, either on Continental or State establishment, and hath been received as a substitute for any free person whose duty or lot it was to serve in such regiment or corps, and hath served faithfully during the term of such enlistment, or hath been discharged from such service by some officer duly authorized to grant such discharge, shall, from and after the passing of this act, be fully and completely emancipated, and shall be held and deemed free, in as full and ample a manner as if each and every of them were specially named in this act ; and the Attorney-general for the Commonwealth is hereby required to commence an action, *in formâ pauperis*, in behalf of any of the persons above described who shall, after the passing of this act, be detained in servitude by any person whatsoever ; and if, upon such prosecution, it shall appear that the pauper is entitled to his freedom in consequence of this act, a jury shall be empanelled to assess ^{Negro} the damages for his detention.

"III. And whereas it has been represented to this General Assembly, that Aberdeen, a negro man slave, hath labored a number of years in the public service at the lead mines, and for his meritorious services is entitled to freedom; *Be it therefore enacted,* That the said slave Aberdeen shall be, and he is hereby, emancipated and declared free in as full and ample a manner as if he had been born free." — *Hening's Statutes at Large of Virginia,* vol. xi. pp. 308, 309.

Negro soldiers emancipated.

Three years after the close of the war, in October, 1786, the following special act was passed, by the General Assembly of Virginia, for the liberation of a faithful slave who had rendered valuable service to General Lafayette : —

"*An Act to emancipate* JAMES, *a Negro Slave, the property of* William Armistead, *Gentleman.*

"I. Whereas it is represented that James, a negro slave, the property of William Armistead, gentleman, of the county of New Kent, did, with the permission of his master, in the year one thousand seven hundred and eighty-one, enter into the service of the Marquis la Fayette, and at the peril of his life found means to frequent the British camp, and thereby faithfully executed important commissions entrusted to him by the Marquis; and the said James hath made application to this Assembly to set him free, and to make his said master adequate compensation for his value, which it is judged reasonable and right to do;

A slave's services to Lafayette acknowledged by Virginia.

"II. *Be it therefore enacted,* That the said James shall, from and after the passing of this act, enjoy as full freedom as if he had been born free; any law to the contrary thereof notwithstanding.

"III. *And be it further enacted,* That the Executive shall, as soon as may be, appoint a proper person, and the said William Armistead another, who shall ascertain and fix the value of the said James, and to certify such valuation to the Auditor of Accounts, who shall issue his warrant to the Treasurer for the same, to be paid out of the general fund." — *Hening's Statutes at Large of Virginia,* vol. xii. pp. 380, 381.

With two or three later authoritative testimonies, showing that it was a general practice among the Founders of the

20

Republic to employ negroes, both slaves and freemen, as soldiers regularly enrolled in the army, I bring to a close this paper, which has already much exceeded the limits of my original plan.

The Hon. William Eustis, who served throughout the war of the Revolution as a surgeon, and was afterwards Governor of Massachusetts, in a speech in the United-States House of Representatives, December 12, 1820, said: —

William Eustis.

"At the commencement of the Revolutionary War, there were found, in the Middle and Northern States, many blacks, and other people of color, capable of bearing arms; a part of them free, the greater part slaves. The freemen entered our ranks with the whites. The time of those who were slaves was purchased by the States; and they were induced to enter the service in consequence of a law, by which, on condition of their serving in the ranks during the war, they were made freemen. In Rhode Island, where their numbers were more considerable, they were formed, under the same considerations, into a regiment commanded by white officers; and it is required, in justice to them, to add, that they discharged their duty with zeal and fidelity. The gallant defence of Red Bank, in which this black regiment bore a part, is among the proofs of their valor.

"Among the traits which distinguished this regiment was their devotion to their officers: when their brave Col. Greene was afterwards cut down and mortally wounded, the sabres of the enemy reached his body only through the limbs of his faithful guard of blacks, who hovered over him and protected him, every one of whom was killed, and whom he was not ashamed to call his children. The services of this description of men in the navy are also well known. I should not have mentioned either, but for the information of the gentleman from Delaware, whom I understood to say that he did not know that they had served in any considerable numbers.

" The war over, and peace restored, these men returned to their respective States; and who could have said to them, on their return to civil life, after having shed their blood in common with the whites in the defence of the liberties of the country, ' You are not to participate in the rights secured by the struggle, or in the liberty for which you have been fighting ' ? Certainly no white man in Massachusetts." — *Annals of Congress. Sixteenth Congress, Second Session,* p. 636.

· The Hon. Charles Pinckney, of South Carolina, in a previous part of the same debate, said: —

. . . "It is a most remarkable fact, that notwithstanding, in the course of the Revolution, the Southern States were continually overrun by the British, and that every negro in them had an opportunity of leaving their owners, few did; proving thereby not only a most remarkable attachment to their owners, but the mildness of the treatment, from whence their affection sprang. They then were, as they still are, as valuable a part of our population to the Union as any other equal number of inhabitants. They were in numerous instances the pioneers, and, in all, the laborers, of your armies. To their hands were owing the erection of the greatest part of the fortifications raised for the protection of our country; some of which, particularly Fort Moultrie, gave, at that early period of the inexperience and untried valor of our citizens, immortality to American arms : and, in the Northern States, numerous bodies of them were enrolled into and fought, by the sides of the whites, the battles of the Revolution." — *Annals of Congress. Sixteenth Congress, First Session*, p. 1312.

That large numbers of negroes were enrolled in the army, and served faithfully as soldiers during the whole period of the War of the Revolution, may be regarded as a well-established historical fact. And it should be borne in mind, that the enlistment was not confined, by any means, to those who had before enjoyed the privileges of free citizens. Very many slaves were offered to, and received by, the army, on the condition that they were to be emancipated, either at the time of enlisting, or when they had served out the term of their enlistment. The inconsistency of keeping in slavery any person who had taken up arms for the defence of our national liberty, had led to the passing of an order, forbidding "slaves," as such, to be received as soldiers.

The documents which I have cited will give a general idea of the opinions and the practice of the leading patriots in the civil and military service of the country, at the time of the Revolution, on the employment of negroes as soldiers. Much more documentary evidence, of a similar character, might be adduced from the mass of materials which I have gathered in pursuing this inquiry; but I have, I trust, selected enough to fairly illustrate the subject. If what I have done, or what I have left undone, shall stimulate others to a more thorough investigation, my labor will not have been lost.

APPENDIX.

APPENDIX.

(A.)

NEGROES IN THE NAVY.

THE suggestion made by Mr. Everett at the meeting of the Massachusetts Historical Society when this paper was read, in regard to the history of the employment of negroes in our navy, is worthy of a more careful consideration than the limits of this paper would allow. But I am happy to be able to present the testimony, on this subject, of one of our Honorary Members, Usher Parsons, M.D., whose character and experience give authority to his statements.

"PROVIDENCE, October 18, 1862.

"MY DEAR SIR, — In reply to your inquiries about the employing of blacks in our navy in the war of 1812, and particularly in the battle of Lake Erie, I refer you to documents in Mackenzie's 'Life of Commodore Perry,' vol. i. pp. 166 and 187.

"In 1814, our fleet sailed to the Upper Lakes to co-operate with Colonel Croghan at Mackinac. About one in ten or twelve of the crews were blacks.

"In 1816, I was surgeon of the 'Java,' under Commodore Perry. The white and colored seamen messed together. About one in six or eight were colored.

"In 1819, I was surgeon of the 'Guerrière,' under Commodore Macdonough; and the proportion of blacks was about the same in her

Negroes in the Navy. crew. There seemed to be an entire absence of prejudice against the blacks as messmates among the crew. What I have said applies to the crews of the other ships that sailed in squadrons.

" Yours very respectfully,

" USHER PARSONS.

" GEORGE LIVERMORE, Esq."

The documents referred to by Dr. Parsons are two letters, — the first written to Commodore Chauncey, in the summer of 1813, by Captain (afterwards Commodore) Perry, expressing dissatisfaction with the appearance of the men who had been sent to him for his squadron on Lake Erie before his famous battle.

" SIR, — I have this moment received, by express, the enclosed letter from General Harrison. If I had officers and men, — and I have no doubt you will send them, — I could fight the enemy, and proceed up the lake ; but, having no one to command the ' Niagara,' and only one commissioned lieutenant and two acting lieutenants, whatever my wishes may be, going out is out of the question. The men that came by Mr. Champlin are a motley set, — blacks, soldiers, and boys. I cannot think you saw them after they were selected. I am, however, pleased to see any thing in the shape of a man." — *Mackenzie's Life of Perry*, vol. i. pp. 165, 166.

This letter called forth from Commodore Chauncey the following sharp reply : —

" SIR, — I have been duly honored with your letters of the twenty-third and twenty-sixth ultimo, and notice your anxiety for men and officers. I am equally anxious to furnish you ; and no time shall be lost in sending officers and men to you as soon as the public service will allow me to send them from this lake. I regret that you are not pleased with the men sent you by Messrs. Champlin and Forrest; for, to my knowledge, a part of them are not surpassed by any seamen we have in the fleet : and I have yet to learn that the color of the skin, or the cut and trimmings of the coat, can affect a man's qualifications or usefulness. I have nearly fifty blacks on board of this ship, and many of them are among my best men: and those people you call soldiers have been to sea from two to seventeen years; and I presume that you will find them as good and useful as any men on board of your vessel; at least, if I can judge by comparison; for those which **Negroes in** we have on board of this ship are attentive and obedient, and, as far as **the Navy.** I can judge, many of them excellent seamen: at any rate, the men sent to Lake Erie have been selected with a view of sending a fair proportion of petty officers and seamen; and I presume, upon examination, it will be found that they are equal to those upon this lake." — *Macken-zie's Life of Perry*, vol. i. pp. 186, 187.

Perry found the negroes to be indeed all that Commodore Chauncey had represented them; and he did not hesitate afterwards to speak favorably of their services: —

" Perry speaks highly of the bravery and good conduct of the negroes, who formed a considerable part of his crew. They seemed to be absolutely insensible to danger. When Captain Barclay came on board the 'Niagara,' and beheld the sickly and party-colored beings around him, an expression of chagrin escaped him at having been conquered by such men. The fresh-water service had very much impaired the health of the sailors, and crowded the sick list with patients." — *Analectic Magazine*, vol. iii. p. 255.

To the same effect is the testimony of the following

" *Extract of a Letter from Nathaniel Shaler, Commander of the private-armed Schooner Gov. Tompkins, to his Agent in New York, dated —*

"AT SEA, Jan. 1, 1813.

. . . . .

" Before I could get our light sails in, and almost before I could turn round, I was under the guns, not of a transport, but of a large *frigate!* and not more than a quarter of a mile from her. . . . . Her first broadside killed two men, and wounded six others. . . . . My officers conducted themselves in a way that would have done honor to a more permanent service. . . . . . The name of one of my poor fellows who was killed ought to be registered in the book of fame, and remembered with reverence as long as bravery is considered a virtue. He was a black man, by the name of John Johnson. A twenty-four-pound shot struck him in the hip, and took away all the lower part of his body. In this state, the poor brave fellow lay on the deck, and several times exclaimed to his shipmates, '*Fire away, my boy: no haul a color down.*' The other was also a black man, by the name of John Davis, and was struck in much the same way. He fell near me, and several times requested to be thrown overboard, saying he was only in the way of others.

"When America has such tars, she has little to fear from the tyrants of the ocean." — *Niles's Weekly Register, Saturday, Feb.* 26, 1814.

(B.)

Flag of a negro company. At the August meeting of the Massachusetts Historical Society, an interesting memorial of the last century was displayed. It was a silk flag, bearing the device of a Pine-tree and a Buck, with the initials "J. H." and "G. W." over a scroll, on which appear the words, "The Bucks of America." This relic had been carefully preserved as the flag presented by Governor Hancock to a company of colored soldiers bearing that name. It now belongs to Mr. William C. Nell, of Boston. Mr. Nell is the author of a volume entitled "The Colored Patriots of the American Revolution, with Sketches of several Distinguished Colored Persons;" a book that contains a great number of interesting anecdotes on the subject. It was published in 1855, and is now out of print; but a new edition, considerably enlarged, is, I am happy to hea.' soon to be issued.

(C.)

NEGRO REGIMENTS IN THE STATE OF NEW YORK.

Negro regiments in the State of New York. That the services of negroes, as soldiers, were solicited and welcomed by the civil and military authorities in various parts of the United States, during the war of 1812 with Great Britain, is too well known to need any illustration. It may not, however, be out of place here to reprint an act of the Legislature of the State of New York.

"An Act to authorize the raising of Two Regiments of Men of Color; passed Oct. 24, 1814.

" SECT. 1. Be it enacted by the people of the State of New York, Negro regiments in represented in Senate and Assembly, That the Governor of the State the State of be, and he is hereby, authorized to raise, by voluntary enlistment, two New York. regiments of free men of color, for the defence of the State for three years, unless sooner discharged.

" SECT. 2. And be it further enacted, That each of the said regiments shall consist of one thousand and eighty able-bodied men; and the said regiments shall be formed into a brigade, or be organized in such manner, and shall be employed in such service, as the Governor of the State of New York shall deem best adapted to defend the said State.

" SECT. 3. And be it further enacted, That all the commissioned officers of the said regiments and brigade shall be white men; and the Governor of the State of New York shall be, and he is hereby, authorized to commission, by brevet, all the officers of the said regiments and brigade, who shall hold their respective commissions until the council of appointment shall have appointed the officers of the said regiments and brigade, in pursuance of the Constitution and laws of the said State.

" SECT. 4. And be it further enacted, That the commissioned officers of the said regiments and brigade shall receive the same pay, rations, forage, and allowances, as officers of the same grade in the army of the United States; and the non-commissioned officers, musicians, and privates of the said regiments shall receive the same pay, rations, clothing, and allowances, as the non-commissioned officers, musicians, and privates of the army of the United States; and the sum of twenty-five dollars shall be paid to each of the said non-commissioned officers, musicians, and privates, at the time of enlistment, in lieu of all other bounty.

" SECT. 5. And be it further enacted, That the troops to be raised as aforesaid may be transferred into the service of the United States, if the Government of the United States shall agree to pay and subsist them, and to refund to this State the moneys expended by this State in clothing and arming them; and, until such transfer shall be made, may be ordered into the service of the United States in lieu of an equal number of militia, whenever the militia of the State of New York shall be ordered into the service of the United States.

" SECT. 6. And be it further enacted, That it shall be lawful for any

Negro regi-
ments in
the State of
New York.

able-bodied slave, with the written assent of his master or mistress, to enlist into the said corps; and the master or mistress of such slave shall be entitled to the pay and bounty allowed him for his service: and, further, that the said slave, at the time of receiving his discharge, shall be deemed and adjudged to have been legally manumitted from that time, and his said master or mistress shall not thenceforward be liable for his maintenance.

"SECT. 7. And be it further enacted, That every such enrolled person, who shall have become free by manumission or otherwise, if he shall thereafter become indigent, shall be deemed to be settled in the town in which the person who manumitted him was settled at the time of such manumission, or in such other town where he shall have gained a settlement subsequent to his discharge from the said service; and the former owner or owners of such manumitted person, and his legal representatives, shall be exonerated from his maintenance, any law to the contrary hereof notwithstanding.

"SECT. 8. And be it further enacted, That, when the troops to be raised as aforesaid shall be in the service of the United States, they shall be subject to the rules and articles which have been or may be hereafter established by the By-laws of the United States for the government of the army of the United States; that, when the said troops shall be in the service of the State of New York, they shall be subject to the same rules and regulations: And the Governor of the said State shall be, and he is hereby, authorized and directed to exercise all the power and authority which, by the said rules and articles, are required to be exercised by the President of the United States." — *Laws of the State of New York, passed at the Thirty-eighth Session of the Legislature,* chap. xviii.

(D.)

GENERAL JACKSON'S PROCLAMATION TO THE NEGROES.

HEADQUARTERS, SEVENTH MILITARY DISTRICT,
MOBILE, September 21, 1814.

To the Free Colored Inhabitants of Louisiana.

Negro sol-
diers under
General
Jackson.

Through a mistaken policy, you have heretofore been deprived of a participation in the glorious struggle for national rights in which our country is engaged. This no longer shall exist.

As sons of freedom, you are now called upon to defend our most inestimable blessing. As Americans, your country looks with confidence to her adopted children for a valorous support, as a faithful return for the advantages enjoyed under her mild and equitable government. As fathers, husbands, and brothers, you are summoned to rally around the standard of the Eagle, to defend all which is dear in existence.

Negro soldiers under General Jackson.

Your country, although calling for your exertions, does not wish you to engage in her cause without amply remunerating you for the services rendered. Your intelligent minds are not to be led away by false representations. Your love of honor would cause you to despise the man who should attempt to deceive you. In the sincerity of a soldier and the language of truth I address you.

To every noble-hearted, generous freeman of color volunteering to serve during the present contest with Great Britain, and no longer, there will be paid the same bounty, in money and lands, now received by the white soldiers of the United States, viz. one hundred and twenty-four dollars in money, and one hundred and sixty acres of land. The non-commissioned officers and privates will also be entitled to the same monthly pay, and daily rations, and clothes, furnished to any American soldier.

On enrolling yourselves in companies, the Major-General Commanding will select officers for your government from your white fellow-citizens. Your non-commissioned officers will be appointed from among yourselves.

Due regard will be paid to the feelings of freemen and soldiers. You will not, by being associated with white men in the same corps, be exposed to improper comparisons or unjust sarcasm. As a distinct, independent battalion or regiment, pursuing the path of glory, you will, undivided, receive the applause and gratitude of your countrymen.

To assure you of the sincerity of my intentions, and my anxiety to engage your invaluable services to our country, I have communicated my wishes to the Governor of Louisiana, who is fully informed as to the manner of enrolment, and will give you every necessary information on the subject of this address.

ANDREW JACKSON, *Major-General Commanding.*

(Niles's Register, vol. vii. p. 205.)

Three months after his proclamation was issued, on Sunday, the 18th of December, 1814, General Jackson reviewed the troops, white and colored, in New Orleans. " At the close of the review, Edward Livingston [one of his aids] advanced from the group that surrounded the General, and read in fine, sonorous tones, and with an energy and emphasis worthy of the impassioned words he spoke, that famous address to the troops which contributed so powerfully to enhance their enthusiasm, and of which the survivors to this hour have the most vivid recollection. This address, like that previously quoted, was Jackson's spirit in Livingston's language." — *Parton's Life of Jackson*, vol. ii. pp. 63, 64.

The following is a portion of the address : —

" To the Embodied Militia. — *Fellow Citizens and Soldiers:* The General commanding in chief would not do justice to the noble ardor that has animated you in the hour of danger, he would not do justice to his own feeling, if he suffered the example you have shown to pass without public notice. . . . . .

" Fellow-citizens, of every description, remember for what and against whom you contend. For all that can render life desirable — for a country blessed with every gift of nature — for property, for life — for those dearer than either, your wives and children — and for liberty, without which, country, life, property, are no longer worth possessing; as even the embraces of wives and children become a reproach to the wretch who could deprive them by his cowardice of those invaluable blessings.

.   .   .   .   .

" To the Men of Color. — Soldiers ! From the shores of Mobile I collected you to arms, — I invited you to share in the perils and to divide the glory of your white countrymen. I expected much from you; for I was not uninformed of those qualities which must render you so formidable to an invading foe. I knew that you could endure hunger and thirst, and all the hardships of war. I knew that you loved the land of your nativity, and that, like ourselves, you had to defend all that is most dear to man. But you surpass my hopes. I have found in you, united to these qualities, that noble enthusiasm which impels to great deeds.

" Soldiers ! The President of the United States shall be informed of your conduct on the present occasion; and the voice of the Representatives of the American nation shall applaud your valor, as your General now praises your ardor. The enemy is near. His sails cover the lakes. But the brave are united; and, if he finds us contending among ourselves, it will be for the prize of valor, and fame its noblest reward." — *Niles's Register*, vol. vii. pp. 345, 346.

(E.)

The Hon. Charles B. Sedgwick, a member of Congress from the State of New York, read in the House of Represen-tatives, during the last session, the following paper on the use of negro soldiers in other countries. It is understood to have been prepared by one of the librarians of the State Library at Albany.

Negro soldiers under monarchical governments.

NEGRO SOLDIERS UNDER MONARCHICAL GOVERNMENTS.

"The monarchical governments of Europe and America, those that tolerate slavery and those that do not, alike agree in employing negroes armed for the public defence. They find that the burdens of war, and the sacrifice of life it occasions, are too great to be borne by the white race alone. They call upon the colored races, therefore, to share in the burden, and to encounter, in common with the whites, the risks of loss of life.

"Thus we find, that in the Spanish colony of Cuba, with a popula-tion one-half slaves and one-sixth colored, a militia of free blacks and mulattoes was directed by Gen. Pezuela (Governor-General) to be organized in 1854 throughout the island; and it was put upon an equal footing, with regard to privilege, with the regular army. This measure was not rescinded by Governor-General Concha in 1855; but the black and mulatto troops have been made a permanent corps of the Spanish army. (Condensed in the very phrases of Thrasher's preface to his edition of Humboldt's ' Cuba.')

"In the Portuguese colonies on the coast of Africa, the regiments are chiefly composed of black men. At Prince's Island, the garrison consists of a company of regular artillery of eighty, and a regiment of black militia of ten hundred and fifty-eight, rank and file, of which the

Negro sol-
diers under
monarchi-
cal govern-
ments. colonel is a white man. At St. Thomas's, there are two regiments of black militia. In Loando, the Portuguese can, on an emergency of war with the natives, bring into the field twenty-five thousand partially civilized blacks, armed with muskets. Successful expeditions have actually been made with five thousand of them, accompanied with three or four hundred white soldiers. (From Valdez's Six Years on the West Coast of Africa. London: 1861. Two vols. 8vo.)

"In the Dutch colony of the Gold Coast of Africa, with a population of one hundred thousand, the garrison of the fortress consists of two hundred soldiers (whites, mulattoes, and blacks), under a Dutch colonel.

"In the capital of the French colony of Senegal, on the same coast, at St. Louis, the defence of the place is in the hands of eight hundred white and three hundred black soldiers. (The preceding facts are also from Valdez.)

"In the Danish island of St. Croix, in the West Indies, for more than twenty-five years past, there have been employed two corps of colored soldiers, in the presence of slaves. (From Tuckerman's Santa Cruz.)

"In Brazil, notwithstanding its three million slaves, its monarchical government employs all colors and races in the military service, either by enlistment or forcible seizure. The police of the city of Rio de Janeiro is a military organization, composed mostly of colored men, drilled and commanded by army officers. The navy is principally manned by civilized aborigines. (Hidder; Ewbank.)

"The course pursued by the British Government in Jamaica, Sierra Leone, and Hindostan, is so notorious, as simply to need to be mentioned.

"In Turkey, no distinction of color or race is made in the ranks of the regular army. Distinction is made, however, on the ground of difference of faith. The army is composed of Mahomedans. Christians and Jews are never recruited. The result is one which the government of Turkey to-day contemplates with alarm. For the last two hundred years, having been frequently engaged in war, her Mahomedan population has been greatly reduced thereby; while her Christian population, at one time greatly inferior in numbers, has now, by peace, so extraordinarily increased, as to bid fair soon to divide the empire. And she dare not now, in her strength, arm them as her soldiers as conscripts, notwithstanding her desire to do it."

(F.)

OMITTED DOCUMENTS.

A brief mention may fitly be here made of some of the documents, alluded to in the prefatory Note, which, on account of the prescribed limits of this publication, have been omitted, and reserved for future use.

1. A despatch from Lord Dunmore to "Secretary the Earl of Hillsborough," dated at Williamsburg, May 1, 1772. The original is in the State-paper Office, London. A manuscript copy was obligingly furnished to me by Mr. Bancroft. It not only corroborates the testimony of the American patriots respecting the antislavery sentiments which prevailed in Virginia prior to the Declaration of Independence, but shows the opinions at that time entertained respecting the relations of slaves to their masters in a time of war, as follows : —

"In case of a war . . . . . the people with great reason tremble at the facility that an enemy would find in procuring such a body of men, attached by no tie to their masters or to the country : on the contrary it is natural to suppose their condition must inspire them with an aversion to both, and therefore are ready to join the first that would encourage them to revenge themselves ; by which means a conquest of this country would inevitably be effected in a very short time."

2. An original letter of Patrick Henry to John Alsop, of Hudson, N.Y., dated at Hanover Court-House, 13 January, 1773, pronouncing slavery to be "as repugnant to humanity as it is inconsistent with the Bible and destructive to Liberty."

3. The laws of some of the Northern and Middle States, at the time of the extinction of slavery therein, making it a penal offence to sell slaves to be taken out of the State without their own consent ; and thus proving the falseness of the charge made by Jefferson Davis and others against the North, of hav-

ing "consulted their own interest by selling their slaves to the South when they prohibited slavery within their limits." My attention has been called to these laws by Professor Lieber.

4. An extract from a letter written to me soon after the publication of the first edition, by Mrs. Lydia Maria Child, in which she shows how admirably successful Lafayette's experiment of emancipation in Cayenne proved in practice. The account is too beautiful and touching to be abridged. I hope hereafter to print it entire.

5. A full and accurate statement of the opinions of that high authority, John Quincy Adams, on the powers of the National Government respecting Slavery and Emancipation in a time of war.

The opponents of Emancipation have recently cited certain Official Papers of his, written when, in the capacity of a diplomatist, he was acting under a slave-holding President and a pro-slavery Administration, and discharging the duties of his office as the Advocate of his government in a controversy between it and a foreign power. It would be wrong to assume that such official papers in every instance necessarily present the personal views of the writer. Indeed, we have on record the following express declaration of Mr. Adams as to one of his official acts: "It was utterly against my wishes; but I was obliged to submit, and prepare the requisite despatches." Such ministerial acts, contrary to his convictions, when he was called on to perform them, were done, to use his own words, in "the bitterness of his heart."

When acting on his own responsibility, in the House of Representatives, in 1836, he made this declaration: —

"From the instant that your slave holding States become the theatre of war, civil, servile, or foreign, from that instant the *war powers of Congress* extend to interference with the institution of slavery in every way in which it can be interfered with, from a claim of indemnity for slaves taken or destroyed, to the cession of the State burdened with slavery to a foreign power."

After years of further reflection, in 1842 he announced, in

the following statement, what he considered as indisputable law : —

"*When your country is actually in war, whether it be a war of invasion or a war of insurrection, Congress has power to carry on the war, and must carry it on according to the laws of war;* and, by the laws of war, an invaded country has all its laws and municipal institutions swept by the board, and martial law takes the place of them."

And the settled opinion of this eminent statesman, in the fulness and maturity of his powers, solemnly reiterated in Congress, was, that, in a time of war, "not only the President of the United States, but the commander of the army, has power to order the universal emancipation of the slaves."

INDEX.

INDEX.

BOSTON:

JOHN WILSON AND SON, STEREOTYPERS AND PRINTERS,

No. 5, WATER STREET.